The Right to Vote

Carole Lynn Corbin

THE
RIGHT
TO
VOTE

Issues in American History

Franklin Watts
New York/London/Toronto
Sydney/1985

Photographs courtesy of:
Culver Pictures, Inc.: pp. 7, 60, 68;
Library of Congress: p. 22;
Schomburg Center for Research in
Black Culture, The New York Public Library,
Astor, Lenox, and Tilden Foundations: pp. 35, 38;
AP/Wide World: p. 53, 95; Sophia Smith Collection
(Women's History Archives): pp. 73, 74;
Illustrator's Stock Photo by Gregg Solomon: p. 86.

Library of Congress Cataloging in Publication Data

Corbin, Carole Lynn.
The right to vote.

(Issues in American history)
Bibliography: p.
Includes index.
Summary: Documents the history of the right to vote in America, from colonial times to the present, including the struggles of blacks, women, and those under twenty-one to win that right.
1. Suffrage—United States—History—Juvenile literature. [1. Suffrage—History] I. Title. II. Series.
JK1846.C67   1985   324.6'2'0973   84-26979
ISBN 0-531-04932-9

Copyright © 1985 by Carole Lynn Corbin
All rights reserved
Printed in the United States of America
5 4 3 2 1

Contents

Introduction
1

Chapter One
Colonial Restrictions on the Vote
5

Chapter Two
The Extension of the Vote
17

Chapter Three
Blacks Win Freedom and the Right to Vote
29

Chapter Four
Blacks Lose the Vote—and Regain It
41

Chapter Five
Women Fight for the Vote
57

Chapter Six
Women Triumph
71

Chapter Seven
The Young Voter
89

For Further Reading
99

Index
101

The Right to Vote

Introduction

Today we view the vote as the cornerstone of our democracy and as our most important right. In *Wesberry v. Sanders* (1964) the Supreme Court declared, "No right is more precious in a free country than that of having a vote in the election of those who make the laws under which . . . we must live." Without the vote we are left with no means except rebellion to prod our legislators to carry out the will of the majority, to guarantee our liberties, and to enforce the Bill of Rights, which grants us the rights to free assembly, free speech, freedom of religion, freedom of the press, and more.

Yet, ironically, despite its importance, the Constitution as written by the Founding Fathers failed to grant us the right to vote. The Constitution mandated when and where federal elections would be held, but it allowed the states to decide who could vote in them. The states often used unethical tactics to deny various groups (like blacks) the right to vote. And because it viewed the provisions of the Constitution narrowly, the Supreme Court allowed the states "legally" to disenfranchise them.

Only demonstrations and demands by the people prodded Congress into passing the laws and/or amendments that made universal suffrage a reality. And that was not until the twentieth century! At that time the Supreme Court reversed its earlier position and ruled that voting is a right that the federal government must protect.

The vote was demanded by the people and was won in piecemeal fashion after long, hard battles that lasted as long as a century for some groups—such as women.

2

The vote was highly prized by those who had fought for it.

Yet the vote is often taken for granted today, and even ignored. The United States has lower voter turnout for national elections than any other democratic country in the world, and even fewer people vote in state and local elections. In the 1984 presidential election only 53 percent of the eligible voters went to the polls.

Sometimes television is accused of reducing the number of voters, primarily because of the early computerized predictions of the winners. On election night in 1980 when Jimmy Carter conceded to Ronald Reagan at 9:50 Eastern Standard Time, newscaster Ted Koppel said, "It's inevitable now that as this night continues that Democrats are simply not going to bother to vote where the polls are still open. Why should they?" Then he realized that there were also congressional elections and said, "Voters on the West Coast, there's more than just a presidential race. Please do vote."

Low voter turnout, however, predates television. Historically, the United States has always had difficulties attracting people to the polls, and beginning with George Washington politicians have had to work to get out the vote. Washington once gave a pre-election-day party and spent fifty pounds—more than the cost of a piece of in-town land—on rum, beer, ginger cakes, roast pork, and other refreshments. Politicians who followed him also offered voters food, drink. And, of course, there were always outright money bribes.

Despite bribes of all types, large numbers of eligible voters have always stayed at home on election day, some because they were unable to travel and others because they were unable to register, but the vast majority because they were uninterested in the election.

3

Today's typical nonvoters fall into one or more categories: the young, the poor, and the uneducated. Generally they feel their votes are useless—that they will not change the election or society.

The nonvoter often does not see that the vote is vital to our democratic system, that it is the means to change not only our political but our entire way of life, and that it is the key to freedom.

1 Colonial Restrictions on the Vote

> We . . . combine ourselves together
> into a civil body politic . . .
> and by virtue hereof do enact,
> constitute and frame such just
> and equal laws . . . as shall be
> thought most meet and convenient
> for the good of the colony. . . .
>
> *Mayflower Compact, 1620*

From the earliest days in our history, groups have attempted to control who votes in order to protect their own interests, frequently religious or economic.

On their way to the New World in 1620 the Puritans on board the *Mayflower* drew up the Mayflower Compact, an agreement to establish a government in Plymouth. Because the document bound the signers to abide by the rules of the majority, it has generally been hailed as the first example of democracy. But well-known historian Marchette Chute has said, "It was not so intended. It was a device, and a remarkable one, to control the majority [by] the minority."

The Puritans were in the minority; the men numbered twenty-one, but they asked only twenty non-Puritans to sign the Compact, which declared that only signers would be allowed to vote in the new colony. That gave the Puritans control over the vote, guaranteeing them the religious freedom they sought. (They had been forced to leave Great Britain because of their break with the Church of England.)

When newcomers settled in Plymouth, they were required to pay a bushel of grain in taxes, but unless they belonged to the Puritan church they were not allowed to vote.

Religious restrictions were most common in the New England colonies, but they existed elsewhere as well; in at least four other colonies Catholics were kept from voting—New York, Maryland, Rhode Island, and South Carolina. Jews were not allowed to vote in most of the colonies. In general, to be allowed to vote during the 1600s a person had to be male, white, twenty-one years old, and Christian, usually Protestant.

By the late 1600s property requirements, which were in accordance with English traditions, were wide-

*The first settlers in Plymouth
sign the Mayflower Compact,
establishing a government for the colony.*

spread. The Massachusetts Bay Colony, which had absorbed Plymouth, and the Connecticut Colony limited the vote to men who were worth forty pounds or who owned land, called a freehold, that provided an income of forty shillings per year.

In both Maryland and Virginia property restrictions also took root, and the requirement to vote was fifty acres of land, a town lot, or valuables worth forty pounds. The property qualifications were stiff, and they lasted over a century. (Originally in Virginia all men over the age of sixteen were allowed to vote because they were all taxed one pound of their "best" tobacco.)

By the beginning of the Revolutionary War era all the thirteen original colonies had passed laws that required a minimum amount of property or personal worth for the right to vote. The laws all stipulated an amount high enough to eliminate voting by owners of small strips of land.

Yet in some colonies a man's personal worth was determined not only by his land or his money, but also by his tools, furniture, slaves, or animals. Thomas Paine, author of the famous Revolutionary War pamphlet *Common Sense*, was therefore prompted to ask if it made sense for a man to lose his right to vote if his mule died, or for a man to gain the right if his mare had a foal.

The vast majority of the colonists, at least until after the Revolutionary War, defended property qualifications because landowners paid the bulk of the taxes. They were also interested in maintaining law and order and believed that penniless voters might be subject to bribery at the polls.

Predictably, however, politicians found a way to get around the voting laws. When Charles Carter ran for the office of burgess (a representative of the elected branch of the legislature) in Virginia in 1736, he was so determined to win that he promised any man who would vote for him half an acre of land in town. Whether or not the man kept his word was no secret, for the vote was by voice and it was the custom for candidates to go to the voting house and thank everyone who voted for them.

Dismayed by this obvious vote buying, the Virginia legislature then passed a law requiring voters to own 50 acres of land, or twenty-five acres with a house on it, or a town lot with a house, or fifty pounds of valuables. That law was thwarted, too. In 1762 for ten shillings a man named Thomas Payne bought a tin shack that had been used to store milk pans, placed it on a lot, and declared himself a homeowner—and a voter. The legislature, naturally, ruled that his vote was illegal and further amended the law, defining a house as having a minimum area of twelve square feet.

Like Virginia, New York raised its property requirements. In 1683 a man had to be worth only forty shillings to vote or had to be a "freeman in any corporation," which gave businessmen the right to vote. The landed gentry complained that "men of no great figure, tailors and other mean conditions" were not only allowed to vote but were even getting elected to office. As a result the legislature upped the property requirement to forty pounds in 1699. The higher amounts in New York and elsewhere also helped to keep new settlers from gaining power and upsetting the status quo, or the way things were.

The voting requirements, especially property ownership, were a way to exclude "undesirables" from voting, but it was not uncommon, especially in Pennsylvania and New York, for the laws to be ignored if the man was well liked and upstanding. In addition, men were often asked to swear to their own worth and they were rarely challenged. Defeated in an assembly election in 1764 in Pennsylvania, Benjamin Franklin blamed his loss on the lies told by "the wretched rabble brought to swear themselves entitled to the vote." During the Revolutionary War, however, Franklin changed his mind about property requirements and supported suffrage for all men, as so many fought the British at great cost.

Yankee ingenuity enabled many young men to get around the voting laws. When the New Jersey assembly wrote its suffrage law in 1725, it specified that only men who owned a freehold worth fifty pounds could vote. In 1776 the requirement was changed from land to any valuables worth fifty pounds, which made it easier for men to meet the voting qualifications. They were asked to swear: "I verily believe I am 21 years of age and worth £50 lawful money." Shortly after the law was relaxed, a penniless young man took the oath and was asked for an explanation. He calmly replied that he valued himself "a great deal more than that." He was allowed to vote, which shows how the determined efforts of a few began to pave the way for universal suffrage.

The land requirements, however, were not as harsh as they sound to today's citizens, for the colonies were prosperous and land was relatively easy to obtain, particulary in the northern and central colonies. William Penn, who founded Pennsylvania as a haven for religious freedom, welcomed newcomers and made it easy to buy land. He charged only five pounds for 100 acres of land, and a man needed only 50 acres to qualify to vote during the 1600s. (The only colony where land was difficult to buy was Virginia, where the king had granted huge tracts of land to a handful of wealthy men.)

To serve in most of the colonial legislatures men had to own much land and/or other property, which kept control of the government in the hands of the landed gentry or rich businessmen; for example, in 1759 the state legislature of South Carolina passed a law stating that only owners of 500 acres of land and ten slaves, and men worth one thousand pounds, were eligible to serve in the state's lower house. Twice as much property was required to be eligible to serve in the upper house. Such requirements for state legislators remained in effect in many places until the 1800s because landowners feared that nonowners, if elected, would impose high land taxes on *them*.

Property and personal worth qualifications to vote came under attack, however, during the Revolutionary War period.

The Revolutionary War Affects Voting
The Declaration of Independence, written in 1776, stated ". . . all men are created equal, that they are endowed by their Creator with certain unalienable Rights, that among these are Life, Liberty and the Pursuit of Happiness. That to secure these rights, Governments are instituted among Men, deriving their just powers from the consent of the governed." Today we generally equate the phrase "from the consent of the governed" with universal suffrage, but what the Founding Fathers had in mind was quite different. They were referring to the men on the voting rolls, the men who met the property or personal worth qualifications.

But during the Revolutionary War many men, especially the soldiers, began to voice objections to the property requirements, and the way was paved for more lenient laws. Two major reasons were cited in support of eliminating the property qualifications. Soldiers were given the right to elect their officers, and in return for their many sacrifices, they wanted the right to elect the men who ran the government. Nonvoters were required to pay taxes, and they took the revolutionaries' rallying cry against Great Britain, "No taxation without representation," and applied it to themselves.

After the colonies broke with England, they needed to write their own state constitutions as (they had been operating under the original charters). Many of them used the opportunity to reduce or eliminate the property requirements for voting.

New Hampshire was the first state to issue its own constitution, and it eliminated the past property requirement—fifty pounds' worth of land—and gave the vote to all taxpayers. That was thought by many at the time to be liberal, even radical or extreme, and only a minority agreed with John Sullivan, who wrote, "No danger can arise to a state from giving the people a free and full voice in their own government." Those who opposed his view came to be labeled conservatives.

Pennsylvania and Georgia also gave the vote to all taxpayers, which caused one Savannah merchant to cry out in anguish that this would "ruin the country."

Some of the states made minor changes in their suffrage requirements; for example, South Carolina reduced its property requirements from 100 acres of land to 50, or a town lot, or their equivalent worth paid in taxes. Substitution of personal valuables or taxes broadened the franchise, especially for businessmen in the cities.

Since the colonists were now divided between the liberals, who wanted to extend the vote, and the conservatives, who wanted to restrict it, some colonies such as North Carolina were forced to write compromise suffrage laws. North Carolina, therefore, allowed all white male taxpayers over the age of twenty-one to vote for representatives to the lower house, but only owners of fifty acres of land were allowed to vote for the state's upper house.

Massachusetts distinguished itself as the only state to raise its property requirement. The increase was defended on the grounds that the price of land and goods had risen, but in fact the delegates had been influenced by John Adams. One of the Founding Fathers and the second president, he was a conservative and was against extending the right to vote because "there will be no end to it. New claims will arise; women will demand the vote; lads from 12–21 will think their rights not enough attended to and every man who has not a farthing will demand an equal voice with any other."

Adams was not alone in his beliefs; a majority of the delegates to the Constitutional Convention, which met in Philadelphia in 1787, favored restricting the vote. Alexander Hamilton said, "The voice of the people has been said to be the voice of God; and however generally it has been quoted and believed, it is not true in fact. The people . . . seldom judge or determine right."

A small but vocal minority, however, argued against the conservatives. Benjamin Franklin said that voting was a right, but his philosophy was just beginning to spread. In general, voting was viewed as a privilege.

Because of the disagreements among the delegates about the role of the people, our government was established on the basis of many compromises. The Founding Fathers created two houses of Congress. The members of the lower house, the House of Representatives, were to be elected directly by the people; members of the upper house, or Senate, were to be elected by the state legislators. It was not until 1913 that the senators were elected directly by the voters. And that required a constitutional amendment, the Seventeenth.

The Founding Fathers thought the selection of the president and vice president too important to be left up to the masses, so they assigned the task to electors from each state, collectively known as the electoral college. The electors were elected or appointed by the state legislators, but after many battles the voters were finally given the right to elect them.

Initially the man who received the highest number of electoral votes became president and one with the second highest became vice president. When that method put men with opposing views—such as John Adams and Thomas Jefferson—in the two highest offices, the electoral college system was amended to allow for separate balloting for each position.

After grappling with the difficult tasks of establishing our form of our government, of setting the terms and qualifications of federal representatives, and of assigning the duties and responsibilities of each of the three branches of government (executive, legislative, and judicial), the Founding Fathers reached an impasse on the question, Who should vote? Some delegates argued against giving men the right to vote in federal elections if they were unable to vote in state elections. Others argued that their constituents would rebel if the national voting requirements were stricter than their state's. Pierce Butler said, "There is no right of which the people are more jealous than that of suffrage." The debates on suffrage were long and bitter, and in the end the delegates decided to allow the states to continue to set their own qualifications. As a result, men who were able to vote in one state were often unable to vote if they moved to another. Eventually, as national elections became as important in men's minds as local ones—and as they realized that through the vote they were able to control the tax rate—they started to demand the right to vote everywhere on the basis that they were citizens. Democracy was about to take hold.

2

The Extension of the Vote

> The revolution of 1800 . . . was as real a revolution in the principles of our government as that of 1776 was in its form; not effected indeed by the sword, as that, but by the rational and peaceable instrument of reform, the suffrage of the people.
>
> *Thomas Jefferson, 1801*

Not granting all citizens the right to vote was one of the few failures of the Founding Fathers. It was a major one, for it caused several bitter battles for the vote in the centuries to come.

During the early 1800s, however, the cause of universal suffrage was aided by the unexpected growth of political parties. The Founding Fathers wanted the best men to serve in government, but they apparently failed to recognize the fact that sharp disagreements would be inevitable once a strong national government was established. It was not long before they found themselves faced with the unwelcome prospect of political parties. When George Washington appointed both Alexander Hamilton and Thomas Jefferson to his Cabinet, they were soon labeled the fighting cocks because they opposed each other at every turn.

Hamilton as secretary of the Treasury instituted policies that favored the wealthy; those who agreed with him united to create the Federalist party. Jefferson, on the other hand, favored policies that would help the common man and supported universal suffrage. Those who joined with Jefferson were known as the Republicans; however, because of their liberal policies they were called democrats by the press, and in time the name of the party was changed to the Democrats.

Toward the end of the eighteenth century, feelings between the two parties grew increasingly hostile. Hamilton was a man unable to withstand criticism, and Jefferson and his supporters launched a massive attack on the Federalists through various newspaper editorials and essays.

When Washington returned in 1796, there was too much hatred of Hamilton for him to run for the presidency so the Federalists' candidate was John Adams. He won, but under the electoral college as it was then set up, Jefferson was elected vice president because he had the second-highest number of votes. (The Twelfth Amendment to the Constitution, adopted in 1804, required the electors to vote for the president and the vice president by separate ballots.)

To add to the awkwardness of the situation, the Federalists, who were in the majority in Congress, passed the unpopular Alien and Sedition Acts. The Alien Act gave the president the power to deport anyone considered "dangerous," and the Sedition Act made it a crime to criticize the government. In effect, the latter wiped out the First Amendment guarantees of freedom of speech and the press. Many Republicans—especially newspaper editors—were arrested, and a Connecticut man was hanged for asking for the right to vote although he would have been allowed to do so in New Hampshire, Pennsylvania, Kentucky, Ohio, or Vermont. In the meantime, Jefferson continued to speak out against the Federalists.

In the bitter presidential election of 1800 between Jefferson and Adams, Jefferson won the popular vote but failed to gain a majority of the electoral votes. According to the Constitutional provisions, it was then up to the House of Representatives to elect the president. The Federalists attempted to elect Aaron Burr, a friend of Jefferson's, but the ploy failed and after thirty-six ballots, Jefferson was declared the winner.

Jefferson's victory was a turning point in our history. It marked the beginning of democracy. The Republicans attempted to extend the vote to all men—not always, however, for purely philosophical reasons. Practically it helped them too, since the "common man" was more likely to vote for them than for the aristocratic Federalists.

In Connecticut the Republicans in the lower house

introduced a bill giving all men the vote, and the Federalists reacted with horror. Noah Webster declared that property owners would be at the mercy of a "merciless gang who have nothing to lose and will delight in plundering their neighbors." The bill was defeated by a vote of 118–58 (or two to one), and the conservatives congratulated themselves.

The Connecticut legislators held off liberalizing the state suffrage law until 1818; they finally caved in because sentiment against the voting restrictions was so high. All white men who served in the militia, paid taxes, and had a "good moral character" were given the vote. But at the same time blacks, except those who had met the property qualifications and who had previously voted, were denied the ballot, or disenfranchised. That was probably due to fear among the whites that many blacks, particularly if the slaves were freed, would move North.

In the new states liberal suffrage laws had been passed without serious opposition. The fourteenth state, Vermont, had won its independence from New York in 1791 and had come into the Union with a suffrage law that gave all white males of "quiet and peaceable behavior" the vote.

Although Congress had imposed strict suffrage laws on the Northwest Territory—ownership of fifty acres of land—all the western states carved out of it except Ohio gave the vote to all men who met the age and residency qualifications. Ohio imposed a taxpayer requirement on the voters, as did Louisiana and Mississippi.

The thirteen original states, primarily ruled by established, conservative men, wanted to hold out against universal suffrage. But when the East became more industrialized and land more difficult to buy, sentiment for it built, and eventually the states gave in.

In Maryland the lower house, the House of Delegates, passed a bill in 1800 that extended the vote to all white men; the bill received fifty-seven votes in favor as opposed to eleven against. But the Senate, which consisted of wealthy men worth a minimum of £100, defeated the bill. Then in 1809, the House of Delegates threatened to call a convention to rewrite the entire state constitution unless the Senate reversed itself and adopted white manhood suffrage; the Senate gave in.

All over the country people were beginning to view the vote as a right. They were not willing to pay taxes without having a strong voice in government. They grumbled that all taxpayers should be entitled to vote, since the colonies had originally broken away from Great Britain to object to "taxation without representation."

Still, suffrage for all men, or manhood suffrage, was not easily won; it was achieved slowly, state by state.

In Massachusetts suffrage reform was debated in 1821. Noting that a voter had to own a freehold that was worth sixty pounds or that provided an income of three pounds per year, Rev. Joseph Richardson said, "The present Constitution would have excluded our Savior from voting." As a compromise between the liberals and the conservatives, the ballot was given to all male taxpayers.

Yet the wealthy politicians found ways to keep control over the government even after all the states had revised their voting laws. Many states were divided into districts that gave the rich conservative areas a higher percentage of representatives than the poorer ones. That tactic, known as gerrymandering, was named after Elbridge Gerry, who was governor of Massachusetts in 1812 and later vice president under James Madison. While Gerry was governor, the Massachusetts legislature—which was controlled by his party—divided the

Elbridge Gerry, the man who as governor of Massachusetts allowed election districts to be drawn in a way that gave the majority party a strong advantage over its opponents—a practice that became known as gerrymandering.

state into election districts that lumped the opposition's strongholds together; this made it impossible for them to win more than a few seats in the legislature. Despite the obvious election rigging—the shape of one district is said to have resembled a prehistoric monster—Gerry signed the bill into law.

Gerrymandering was not declared illegal by the Supreme Court until the 1960s. First the Supreme Court ruled in the landmark case *Baker* v. *Carr* (1962) that the courts could hear cases in which the appointment of representatives was challenged. Later, the Supreme Court ruled that election districts have to be set up so that each has approximately the same number of voters. (In some states the districts had been so lopsided that one would have 10,000 voters and another 3,000, but each would have one representative. The Court established what is known as the one man, one vote principle.

During the 1800s divisions between the rural areas and the cities became factors in the suffrage debates. In New York there was a split between the farmers, who feared heavy land taxes, and the new industrial class—the tradesmen and the factory workers. At the state constitutional convention in 1821, John Cramer argued in favor of giving working men the vote. He said, "[They] add to the substantial wealth of the nation in peace. These are the men who constitute your defense in war. . . . Men who in defense of their liberties, and to protect the property of this country, have hazarded their lives; and who, to shield your wives and children from savage brutality; have faced the destructive cannon. All this they could be trusted to do . . . but [some will not] trust them with tickets at the ballot boxes." His view prevailed to the extent that all taxpayers, militiamen, and roadworkers were enfranchised, yet the law was still unpopular because it did not include all workers. Volunteer fire fighters, for example, were exempt from taxes because of the nature of their work, and were not named as voters.

In 1824, when he ran for governor of New York, DeWitt Clinton promised he would fight for suffrage reform. He said, "Without the rights of suffrage, liberty cannot exist. It is a vital principle of representative government." He won, and within months suffrage was given to all white males who had been residents of the state for at least a year; blacks worth at least £250 were also given the vote. At the same time the New York legislators passed a law giving the voters the right to select the presidential electors; previously, the legislature had appointed or selected them. All of the states had given the people this same right except South Carolina and Delaware.

The reform in the electoral college system followed the bitter election of 1824 between Andrew Jackson and John Quincy Adams. Jackson won the popular vote, but he failed to win a majority of the electoral votes and the House of Representatives voted for Adams. In the next election Jackson was determined to win by a wide margin, and through the newspapers he urged the "common man" to go to the polls. They did; 250 percent more people went to the polls than in 1824, and Jackson won easily. A hero of the War of 1812 and a supporter of economic suffrage and reform, Jackson was widely viewed, even by his critics, as a "friend of the people."

Jackson ushered in an era of reform, known as the period of Jacksonian Democracy. Such things as free public education and expanded suffrage were demanded by the people, and Jackson supported them.

Unfortunately Jackson was powerless to extend the

franchise himself. He encouraged the last holdouts to reform their suffrage laws, yet states like Virginia and Rhode Island bitterly resisted the trend towards democracy. Virginia's first concession to the nonvoters was small; in 1829 leaseholders and householders who paid taxes were given the right to vote, but it took another twenty-one years before all white males were enfranchised. Rhode Island, the smallest state, was one of the first to become industrialized, but it had one of the stiffest property requirements: £100 worth of "lands, tenements or hereditaments." Here the fight over suffrage led to an armed rebellion.

Although he was personally a wealthy landowner, radical Thomas Dorr took on the battle of the nonvoters and founded the Rhode Island Suffrage Association in 1840. Within six months there were chapters of the organization in almost every town in the state. They met on April 17, 1841, and called it People's Day. They wore badges that read, "I am an American citizen." The people of Rhode Island wanted the same right—the vote—that the people of Kentucky, New York, Indiana, and other states enjoyed. It was a dramatic demonstration showing that the people had come to equate the right to vote with citizenship even though the Constitution, at that time, had not given anyone the right to vote.

In October, Dorr led a People's Convention, and at it a constitution was written and an election day set. The members of the suffrage organization elected Dorr governor of the state in April 1842, but the Rhode Island General Assembly naturally ignored the election, calling it "foolish nonsense."

Dorr and his followers then stormed the governor's mansion, and the governor called out the militia. In the scuffle that followed several people were arrested, but

Dorr managed to escape. When he returned to the state of his own free will, in 1843, he was arrested and charged with treason.

In his defense Dorr said, "The servants of a righteous cause may fail or fall in the defense of it. . . . But all the truth that it contains is indestructible." His philosophy fell on deaf ears, and he was found guilty. He was sentenced to hard labor for life, which outraged the public so much that the next governor was pressured into releasing him.

Ironically, the year before Dorr's sentencing, the Rhode Island legislators had extended the franchise to all those who were native-born and who paid a one dollar tax, a poll tax; for the foreign-born the property requirement stood.

The legislators were reacting to the tremendous influx of immigrants to the United States, especially along the eastern seaboard. By 1830, over half a million immigrants had entered the country, and the often noisy, uneducated, penniless newcomers were rarely welcomed. As a result, many states attempted to pass suffrage requirements that would shut out the immigrants; the most common method was a residency requirement, usually one or two years.

Other devices to keep the immigrants from casting their ballots included literacy tests—in order to vote they had to be able to read and write, and sometimes they had to explain the meaning of sections in either the state or the national constitution. Although literacy tests became notorious for keeping blacks from voting in the South, they were actually used first in the Northeast. Connecticut adopted literacy tests in 1855, Massachusetts in 1857, and Maine in 1892. Following their lead, some western states like California used literacy tests to keep Orientals from voting.

Thus suffrage was not universal in the 1800s; the number of voters had increased dramatically, but all women and almost all blacks were excluded from the vote. The next major suffrage battles would be theirs.

3
Blacks Win Freedom and the Right to Vote

> Our people were emancipated in a whirl of passion, and then left naked to the mercies of their enraged and impoverished ex-master. As our sole means of defence we were given the ballot, and [then it] was taken from us by force and fraud.
>
> *National Negro Committee, 1895*

While the antislavery, or abolitionist, movement was growing in the United States during the early and mid-1800s, the free blacks were subjected to new laws that stripped them of their rights and the ballot. When the inevitable end to slavery was clear, many whites panicked.

Laws known as the Black Codes were passed, primarily in the South but also in several western states such as Kansas. The Black Codes forbade blacks to meet in groups even for church services, required them to carry papers proving they were free, and banned them from living in many areas. Blacks were required to pay taxes, but their children were not permitted to attend public schools; they were forbidden to join the military although many blacks had served courageously in the Revolutionary War and the War of 1812. They were not allowed to testify in court, and in 1859 Arkansas went so far as to pass a law that required a free black to leave the state or choose a master.

Free blacks also lost the right to vote in most of the states where they still had it. Until the mid-1700s, free blacks, who numbered only 50,000 out of 700,000, were allowed to vote in all the colonies except South Carolina and Georgia as long as they met the property requirements. During the Revolutionary War period when the states wrote their constitutions, many (such as Virginia) excluded blacks from the vote. Then the ballot was taken away from blacks in Delaware, Maryland, Pennsylvania, North Carolina, and Connecticut; in Connecticut; however, blacks already on the voting rolls were not removed. Except for Vermont and Maine, no state that entered the Union gave blacks the vote until after the Civil War.

At the start of the Civil War, blacks were unable to vote everywhere except in five northern states where only 6 percent of them lived—Maine, Vermont, New Hampshire, Rhode Island, and Massachusetts. The expression "free, white, and twenty-one" was a popular one, and it summed up the plight of the blacks.

Denying blacks their rights was generally defended on the grounds that they were inferior to whites. Even the liberal and intellectual magazine *The Nation* wrote that "the average intelligence among [blacks] is very low—so low that they are slightly above the level of animals." What critics of blacks failed to note was that almost all blacks were barred from getting an education; in some states, such as South Carolina, teaching slaves to read and write was a crime punishable by death.

The real reason that blacks were stripped of their rights was that it was economically better for whites in both the North and the South. In the North the period of disenfranchisement for blacks coincided with an influx of European immigrants into the industrial areas, where poor whites competed with blacks for the same jobs. In the South the wealthy plantation owners were interested in maintaining the slave system and their way of life.

Nevertheless, the problems of free blacks—even their lack of rights—were minor in comparison to the problem of obtaining freedom for the slaves, who numbered about 4,000,000.

The Aftermath of the Civil War
In 1863, during the Civil War, Abraham Lincoln issued the Emancipation Proclamation, which freed the slaves in the Confederate states: South Carolina, Mississippi, Florida, Alabama, Georgia, Louisiana, Texas, Virginia, Arkansas, North Carolina, Tennessee, Kentucky, and Missouri.

At the close of the Civil War, the Thirteenth Amendment to the Constitution freed all the slaves. But the Southern states lost no time at all in passing even tougher Black Codes, and with no money, no homes, and no property, thousands of blacks wandered the South and were often beaten or arrested. Carl Schurz, a Union general, reported that "violent efforts were made by white people to drive the . . . Negroes back to the plantations by force. I saw . . . women as well as men, whose ears had been cut off or whose bodies were slashed with knives or bruised with whips or bludgeons, or punctured with shot wounds."

Black leader Frederick Douglass repeatedly told abolitionists, "Slavery is not abolished until the black man has the ballot. While the Legislatures of the South retain the right to pass laws making discrimination between black and white, slavery still lives there."

Yet President Lincoln favored policies that gave the South the freedom to reestablish their own state governments. He was also against forcing the states to give blacks the vote, and as a result, the Southern states returned many of the same men to office who had served in Congress before the Civil War. These politicians held the Republicans responsible for the freeing of the slaves and the destruction of the plantation system. Unless blacks were allowed to vote, it was unlikely that the Republicans would win representatives from the Confederate states; that, in turn, meant they would not be able to retain their majority in Congress.

After Lincoln's assassination Vice President Andrew Johnson took over in the White House, and Republicans expected him to "punish" the South. He stunned them by saying, "I do not want [the Southerners] to come back into the Union a degraded . . . people."

The radical Republicans, or left wing of the party, then refused to allow the Confederates to take their seats in Congress and pushed the Civil Rights Act of 1866 through Congress. Essentially the bill said that the ex-slaves were citizens and were entitled to all the rights of citizens.

Johnson, a supporter of states' rights, vetoed the bill, saying it would be "worse than madness" to give blacks the opportunity to "rule the white race . . . and shape the destiny of the whole country."

Congress overrode his veto, and to prevent repeal of the bill in the future, it passed the Fourteenth Amendment to the Constitution: "All persons born or naturalized in the United States, and subject to the jurisdiction thereof, are citizens of the United States and of the state wherein they reside. No state shall make or enforce any law which shall abridge the privileges or immunities of citizens." That section was written to protect blacks from the harsh Black Codes.

The Fourteenth Amendment fell short of giving blacks the vote, but its second section called for the reduction of congressional representation for any state that denied blacks the right to vote. That attempt to get the states to enfranchise blacks failed, however, because it was never enforced.

The Southern states naturally rejected the Fourteenth Amendment. To put pressure on them Congress passed the Reconstruction Act of 1867, which divided the South into five districts and placed them under martial, or military, law. It also required all the Confederate states except Tennessee (the only one to ratify the Fourteenth Amendment) to rewrite their state constitutions. Delegates to the constitutional conventions were to be elected by male citizens of "whatever race." Congress gave blacks the opportunity to vote, anticipating that the new constitutions would give them suffrage for all elections, which would mean electing state legislators likely to ratify the amendment. Blacks were elected to all the state constitutional conventions. However, in proportion to the black population their percentage was low except in South Carolina, where they were in the majority.

The provisions of the constitutions were hotly debated, none more so than suffrage. Many whites argued that blacks, because most of them lacked an education, were not qualified to vote intelligently.

Beverly Nash, a black delegate in South Carolina, said, "[Blacks] are not prepared for this suffrage. But we can learn. Give a man tools and let him commence to use them, and in time he will learn a trade. So it is with voting. We may not understand it at the start, but in time we shall learn to do our duty."

In general the Southern state constitutions that emerged were progressive; they extended the vote to all men and even eliminated property requirements to hold elected office. They abolished prison sentences for debts, they made unused land available to both blacks and whites—which was vital to the ex-slaves—and they established free public schools.

By the end of 1867 over 700,000 blacks had registered to vote in the South, a number that even in the North was viewed with alarm and disgust. The *New York Times* said in an editorial, "The blacks have been made citizens before they are fit for the responsibilities of electors."

Within three years there were more registered black voters than white in Alabama, Louisiana, Florida, Mississippi, and South Carolina. In Georgia the number of black voters equaled the number of white ones.

The Reconstruction Act of 1867 gave black men such as these freed slaves in New Orleans the right to vote for the first time.

Ironically, several Northern states, including Connecticut, Wisconsin, Kentucky, Ohio, Michigan, and New York, had debated black suffrage but none had enacted it. At the 1860 New York State Constitutional Convention, Frederick Douglass had said, "It is a mockery to talk about protection in a government like ours to a class in it denied the elective franchise. The very denial of that right strips them of 'protection,' and leaves them at the mercy of all that is low, vulgar, cruel and base in the community. The ballot box and the jury box both stand closed against the man of color. . . . The white people of this country would wade knee deep in blood before they would be deprived of either."

It was not until Congress passed the Fifteenth Amendment that discrimination against black voters was finally abolished throughout the country: "The right of citizens of the United States to vote shall not be denied or abridged by the United States or by any state on account of race, color or previous condition of servitude." The amendment was ratified, after many long battles, in 1870. It marked a turning point in the history of voting because the federal government, instead of the states, had become the vehicle for extending suffrage.

Later that year the first black, Hiram R. Revels of Mississippi, was elected to the Senate; he was seated after heated debate. Joseph H. Rainey of South Carolina was elected as the first black member of the House of Representatives, but throughout the Reconstruction period, which lasted from 1867 to 1880, only sixteen blacks actually served in Congress; others had been elected but not allowed to take their seats.

On the state and local levels more blacks were elected, giving rise to unfounded rumors that illiterate blacks had taken over the Southern legislative houses and local governments. In fact, blacks were in a majority only in the upper house of South Carolina's legislature, and the blacks who were elected were, for the most part, intelligent and informed.

But prejudice was rampant, and from the moment blacks were given the right to vote there were those determined to block them. Polling places were moved without notice, roads into town were "out of repair" on election days, ballot boxes were stuffed, and bribery was widespread. Most of all, however, blacks were intimidated by violence.

Throughout the 1870s white racist organizations like the Knights of the White Camelia, the Pale Faces, and the Ku Klux Klan, mushroomed. They attacked blacks who attempted to vote, they destroyed black schools and harassed the teachers, they burned black houses and crops, they warned black officials to resign or face "justice," and they beat and lynched blacks almost at will. Congressional hearings on the violence directed against blacks filled thirteen volumes.

In response to the terrorism of the white racists, Congress passed the Enforcement Acts of 1870–71, popularly called the Ku Klux Klan Acts. They gave the president the power to send federal troops into the Southern states to enforce the peace, and they prohibited state election officials from discriminating against blacks. But President Ulysses S. Grant hesitated to use federal troops and when he did, they, too, were often threatened and driven out of town.

Because of the long list of laws such as the Civil Rights Act of 1866 and the Ku Klux Klan Acts that the Republicans had forced on the South, thousands of whites deserted the party; by the 1870s it was impossible for a white Southerner to become a Republican without also becoming a social outcast.

Racist groups like the White League used the threat of violence to prevent blacks from voting in the South.

The Democrats kept blacks out of the party, claiming it was a private organization, and in the South it was soon "lily white." By 1876 the Democrats controlled all the Southern state houses except those in South Carolina, Louisiana, and Florida. Soon they controlled those, too, since they often blocked the entrances to polling places to prevent blacks from voting, or stole Republican ballot boxes, or moved the polls without warning. The South Carolina Democratic Party advised its members, "Every Democrat must feel honor-bound to control the vote of at least one Negro, by intimidation, purchase, keeping him away or as each individual may determine, how he may best accomplish it."

In the late nineteenth century, it was not a simple matter for a man—in the North *or* the South—to cast a vote according to his conscience and his beliefs. Unlike today, there were neither voting machines nor secret ballots; the paper ballots used in the 1800s were printed by the political party, and everyone knew for whom a person had voted. Secret ballots did not become common until 1890, thus whites who voted for Republicans were easily identified and subjected to the same violent tactics as blacks. As black representative Johan Lynch of Mississippi said, "The outlook for the colored man was dark and anything but encouraging." The picture was about to get even darker.

In 1876 two events further eroded the rights of blacks. The first was the contested election between Republican Rutherford B. Hayes and Democrat Samuel J. Tilden. Hayes "stole" the election from Tilden, who won the popular vote, for in three states—Louisiana, South Carolina, and Florida—Republican election boards oversaw the voting and returned a set of results that showed Hayes the winner. The Democrats, claiming fraud, returned a second set. The contested votes were necessary to determine the presidential winner, and the House of Representatives was forced to decide which votes to count. The House was deadlocked for four months, and fear grew that the nation would be plunged into chaos. Then Hayes offered to remove the federal troops from the South in return for the Southern Democrats' votes. Hayes was elected, and as he had promised, he withdrew the troops and left blacks without federal protection. Blacks lived with violence or the threat of it every day, and they soon lost all their rights—including the vote.

The final blow to black civil rights came from the Supreme Court. In a series of decisions the Court ruled that voting was not an automatic right of citizens and that the states were empowered by the Constitution to establish their own voting regulations. Soon "white supremacy" took firm root in the South as Southern legislatures were given a free rein to find ways to take away the blacks' right to vote—"legally." The Court also ruled that separate facilities for blacks were legal if they were equal to those for whites, thus allowing segregation to exist.

Frederick Douglass scathingly denounced the setbacks suffered by blacks: "The workshop denies him work, the inn denies him shelter; the ballot-box a fair vote, the jury-box a fair trial. He has ceased to be the slave of an individual, but has in some sense become the slave of society."

4 Blacks Lose the Vote —and Regain It

> Give us the ballot and
> we will no longer have to
> worry the federal government
> about our basic rights.
>
> *Martin Luther King, Jr., 1964*

By the turn of the twentieth century, voting was little more than a memory for the vast majority of blacks in the South. In an important case in 1876, *United States* v. *Cruikshank,* the Court had paved the way for the South's "legal" disenfranchisement of blacks. The Court ruled that voting was not a right of citizens and that the states were free to set their own suffrage requirements, just as they had done in the past. Now, however, the suffrage restrictions had to be applied to everyone because the Fifteenth Amendment to the Constitution had outlawed voter discrimination.

After the ruling the first state to rewrite its constitution's suffrage sections was Mississippi. Its new voting law required voters to pay a poll tax and to pass a literacy test, which consisted of being able to read or write any section of either the federal or state constitution. From 1890 to 1920 all the Southern states except Texas and Arkansas passed their own versions of literacy tests. Several other states, including Connecticut and New York, also adopted literacy tests in order to keep immigrants from voting.

The Battle Over Literacy Tests
In 1898 literacy tests were challenged in the Supreme Court in the *Williams* v. *Mississippi* case, but they were declared legal because they were supposed to apply to both blacks and whites. That decision set a precedent that was very difficult to overturn and that all but ended black voting in the South.

The literacy tests were given orally, which gave the all-white registrars tremendous power. They were able to ask whatever they wanted, and blacks were often asked such ridiculous questions as "How many feathers does a chicken have?" Sometimes they were asked such difficult questions about the constitution that even lawyers would not have been able to answer. As a result, college-educated blacks often "failed" while illiterate whites "passed."

The literacy tests had a devastating effect on black voter registration; for example, 130,000 blacks were registered to vote in Louisiana in 1893; after the literacy tests were instituted the number of black voters dropped to 5,000. The pattern was the same throughout the South.

There was little pretense among Southern legislators that the literacy tests were designed to promote intelligent voting. They often bragged about the "legal" disenfranchisement of blacks. Their attitude was summed up by J. K. Vardaman: "I am just as opposed to Booker Washington [a well-educated black leader] . . . as a voter, . . . as I am to the coconut-headed, chocolate-colored [boy] who blacks my shoes every morning. Neither is fit to perform the supreme function of citizenship."

In Louisiana the legislators went one step further than requiring literacy tests; they exempted anyone whose forebears had voted on or before January 1, 1867, from having to take the tests. This was called the grandfather clause, and it was adopted by some other states as well.

The National Association for the Advancement of Colored People (NAACP) was founded in 1909 by black leaders like W. E. B. Du Bois primarily to fight against unfair suffrage laws. Du Bois said, "with the right to vote goes everything: Freedom, manhood, the honor of your wives, the chastity of your daughters, the right to work, and the chance to rise, and let no man listen to those who deny this."

The NAACP also brought suit against "Jim Crow"

laws, which were named after a blackface minstrel character who danced about to the lyrics, "Weel a-boutt and turn a-bout! And . . . jump . . . Jim Crow." Basically the Jim Crow laws mandated segregation.

Although the NAACP wanted to pursue the fight for equal rights through the courts, it was a difficult process; however, they won a minor victory in 1915 in *Guinn v. United States,* when the Supreme Court ruled that grandfather clauses were illegal. It was obvious, the Court declared, that they were designed to prevent blacks from voting; in the same ruling, however, the Court declared that literacy tests, because on the books they applied to everyone, *were* legal.

Literacy tests remained on the lawbooks, and it was not until 1948 that the Supreme Court struck its first blow at such tests, in a suit brought against Alabama by the NAACP and the Voters and Veterans Association (VVA). The Court found that Alabama had used the tests, which were oral, in a discriminatory manner, but it also ruled that a "uniform, objective standardized test" could be given. Written tests were then adopted, holding the hope of fairness, but blacks were still subjected to discrimination because they were often kept waiting hours and even days before they were given the tests. They were also ruled ineligible to vote because of minor errors in filling out forms, or they were not notified about their scores until after the elections.

Even in the few places where blacks were given a fair chance to take the test, they were at a great disadvantage. Nearly 45 percent of all blacks over the age of twenty-five had had less than four years of formal schooling, compared to fifteen percent of whites. Additionally, black schools were generally below the standards of white ones. In *Plessy v. Ferguson* in 1896, the

Supreme Court had ruled that separate facilities for blacks—including schools—were legal if they were "equal" to those for whites; in reality, of course, they never were. That inequality, however, was not proved to the Court's satisfaction until *Brown* v. *Board of Education of Topeka* in 1954, when it ruled that the "separate but equal" doctrine was inherently unfair.

In the meantime, literacy tests remained in effect. Even as late as 1959 the Supreme Court ruled that "the ability to read and write has some relation to standards designed to promote intelligent use of the ballot." Yet the tests were not used everywhere, so whether or not a person qualified to vote depended upon the state in which he or she lived.

Literacy tests were finally banned by the Voting Rights Act of 1965, which suspended them in all elections where less than fifty percent of all eligible voters were registered.

Poll Taxes
Like literacy tests, poll taxes were passed in the South to make it very difficult for blacks to vote. (Ironically, poll taxes were first charged in New Hampshire in 1776 as a means of expanding the vote for all. Taxpayers were given the ballot under the new suffrage law, and the poll tax was a way for all men to meet this requirement.) The poll tax was a suffrage reform that was distorted by the racists. On the surface, the Southern states' nominal poll taxes of $1.50 or $2.00 did not seem significant, but the gimmicks attached to them effectively disenfranchised black voters. For example, in Mississippi the tax had to be paid months in advance, and the receipt was supposed to be presented at the polls, but only blacks were required to show it.

As early as 1898 in *Williams* v. *Mississippi,* a case that also challenged literacy tests, the poll tax was contested, but the Supreme Court ruled it was constitutional because everyone was required to pay it, black or white. Once the Court handed down that decision, other states including Louisiana, North Carolina, Virginia, Georgia, Alabama, Florida, and Oklahoma jumped on the bandwagon and passed similar laws.

As the years went by, poll taxes were attacked by poor whites, liberals, and union workers; and they were also opposed by such organizations as the American Federation of Labor (AFL), the YWCA, and the United Jewish Youth League. Some states responded to the opposition—North Carolina dropped its poll tax in 1920, and during the Depression, Louisiana and Florida dropped theirs (1934 and 1937).

During and after World War II the poll tax came under fire because even soldiers were required to pay it. As a gesture of goodwill, Mississippi exempted veterans, but when black veterans lined up to get their exemption certificates, they were driven off by mobs of angry whites.

On the national level, demand grew for a federal law outlawing poll taxes. The House of Representatives passed several such bills between 1942 and 1949, but all of them were killed in the Senate, even though 63 percent of the people, according to a Gallup survey, opposed the poll tax.

Senate Southern Democrats opposed the banning of the poll tax because they feared it would set a precedent for the banning of other suffrage requirements, such as literacy tests. They feared that the states would lose their power to establish their own voting qualifications, and that they would have to allow blacks to vote.

Opponents of poll taxes brought suits against them, but time after time the Supreme Court ruled that they were legal. Finally, in 1960, after a massive civil rights movement, Congress passed the Twenty-Fourth Amendment to the Constitution: "The right of citizens of the United States to vote in any primary or other election for President or Vice President, for electors for President or Vice President, or for Senator or Representative in Congress, shall not be denied or abridged by the United States or any State by reason of failure to pay any poll tax or other tax."

The amendment was passed in 1962 and ratified in 1964, but it affected only federal elections. Alabama, Arkansas, Mississippi, Texas, and Virginia—the only states where poll taxes were still charged—continued to collect them for local and state elections. In 1966 the Supreme Court reversed itself and declared all poll taxes illegal based on the Fourteenth Amendment.

The White Primary
Between 1896 and 1915 all the former Confederate states, along with Oklahoma, passed laws that gave political parties the freedom to accept or reject whomever they wanted, thus giving them a third way to keep blacks from gaining political power.

As noted earlier, by the turn of the century most whites belonged to the Democratic party because the Republicans had freed the slaves and had pushed through the various Reconstruction laws. Blacks had voted almost exclusively for the Republicans and had been kept out of the Democratic party through violence and intimidation.

Once blacks had lost their right to vote through the passage of laws mandating literacy tests and poll taxes, one-party control by the Democrats made the primaries, or elections to nominate the party's candidate, the true elections. The winner of the Democratic primary was sure to be elected in the general elections. Since only registered party members were allowed to vote in the primaries, the "white primary" proved to be another obstacle for blacks seeking the vote.

The legality of the white primary was challenged before the Supreme Court several times, but the Court agreed with the states' position that political parties were private and voluntary and therefore free to choose their own members. For years the Court ignored the question of whether or not primaries are elections—subject to the Fifteenth Amendment, which forbids discrimination in voting.

At the Southern Negro Youth Conference in May 1938, a position paper stated, "It is as important . . . that we win the right to vote in the party primaries as in the general elections because in most sections of the South victory in the Democratic primary is synonymous with election. This right can only be secured when the United States Supreme Court reverses its decision which held the primaries to be private affairs. The recent addition of liberal judges to the bench [Benjamin M. Cardozo, appointed to the Supreme Court in 1932, and Hugo Black, appointed in 1937, later supported civil rights legislation] may bring a reversal if somehow a new primary case can be presented."

That opportunity came in 1941 with *United States* v. *Classic*, when the Court declared that primaries are elections if they are "integral" to the political system. That case set a precedent; when Lonnie Smith, a black Houston dentist, was denied the right to vote in the 1940 Democratic primary in Texas, he sued the voting registrar, proved the primary was "integral," and won the case. The Supreme Court had finally put the white primary to death.

Civil Rights Legislation
Although the Supreme Court had finally declared the grandfather clauses and the white primary unconstitutional, there were still other barriers to keep blacks from voting in the South, including literacy tests and terrorist tactics. Over the years the NAACP and other groups filed thousands of complaints with Congress citing instances where blacks had been beaten, mutilated, whipped, tarred, or even killed to prevent them from exercising their rights. The federal government, however, contended that it was unable to intervene, as anyone accused of assault, manslaughter, or murder had to be tried in his or her own state. In the South white juries rarely, if ever, convicted fellow whites accused of attacking blacks, so violence kept blacks at home on election day.

Increasingly, blacks began to demand federal legislation that would protect them and ensure their rights, particularly after World War II. When so many blacks had distinguished themselves on the battlefield fighting for democracy, they now demanded that democracy be carried out at home. Because they had moved to the North in significant numbers and had tended to cluster in large cities like New York or Chicago, that concentration had given them more political power. They had begun to influence, if not to change, many elections including the presidential one.

Then, in 1954, the Supreme Court handed down the historic *Brown* v. *Board of Education* ruling declaring "separate but equal" schools unconstitutional. The Court ordered the integration of schools "with all deliberate speed." That decision hit the nation, and especially the South, like a bombshell. Violence erupted in the streets, North and South, and touched off a massive civil rights movement. The obvious discrimination against blacks aroused the conscience of the nation, and more and more people supported a national bill to protect the rights of all.

Despite strong opposition from Southern Democrats, Congress passed the Civil Rights Act of 1957. Among its provisions was one that gave the U.S. attorney general the right to go to court to enforce the voting laws.

When John F. Kennedy was elected president in a very tight race in 1960, he owed a debt to the blacks who had supported him and helped to put key states like New Jersey, New York, and Illinois into his column. He appointed his brother Robert attorney general and directed him to bring suit against many registrars in the South accused of discriminating against blacks. Robert Kennedy did bring many of them to court, but the cases were often thrown out because the registrars had resigned; in many other instances they had destroyed the voting records, and he had no evidence to press the case.

It was clear that the Civil Rights Bill of 1957 was flawed and that a stronger bill was needed to protect black rights. It was just as clear that Southern Democrats planned to block it, and they did everything possible to delay it or water it down. The bill was kept in committee for weeks before being released for floor debate.

After a heated battle, the Civil Rights Bill of 1960 was passed, and it remedied the major faults of the 1957 law. It allowed the federal government to sue the state if the registrar resigned, and it required all local and state governments to preserve voting records for twenty-two months. That gave the federal government the ammunition needed to protect blacks' voting rights. Over 600,000 blacks registered to vote for the first time in the two-year period from 1962 to 1964. But nearly all of the new voters were in Tennessee, Florida, and Texas; in the Deep South only 40 percent of the eligible blacks registered because of continued violence.

To prod Congress into passing a stiffer civil rights bill and putting an end to terrorism, black leaders such as Martin Luther King, Jr., Bayard Rustin, and A. Philip Randolph organized a march on Washington, D. C. On August 28, 1963, over 200,000 blacks and whites demonstrated to insist on equal rights for all. The next year, after overcoming Southern efforts to prevent it, the most far-reaching civil rights bill to date was passed. It called for the integration of public accomodations, made a sixth-grade education proof of literacy (though literacy tests were still legal), and sent "voter referees" into the South to register voters.

Black organizations like the Student Non-Violent Coordinating Committee (SNCC), the Southern Christian Leadership Conference (SCLC), and the NAACP led voter registration drives all over the country, especially in the Deep South. Despite such efforts, there were counties where a minuscule number of blacks were registered. Dallas County, Alabama, was one of these; only 2 percent, or 383 blacks, were registered there, and Martin Luther King, Jr. made it his target for a registration drive, touching off confrontations between whites and blacks that left the country reeling.

In Selma, King led a group to the registration office; they were met by a vicious mob and driven off.

Undeterred, King planned a march from Selma to the state capital of Montgomery to show how determined the blacks were to vote. Originally planned to begin on March 7, the march was delayed more than once because of violence. It finally began on March 21 under the protection of federal troops. By then hundreds of black and white civil rights advocates who had gathered in Selma had been arrested on minor charges. The marchers had been beaten with nightsticks, pelted with bottles and debris, jabbed with cattle prods, and blasted with fire hoses. Several had even been killed, and the conscience of the nation had been aroused.

President Lyndon B. Johnson pressured Congress into passing the highly controversial Voting Rights Bill of 1965 soon after the march. Signed into law on August 6, 1965, it finally paved the way for blacks to regain their right to vote in the South—almost a century after they had been given that right by the Fifteenth Amendment.

Basically, the Voting Rights Bill suspended literacy tests wherever less than 50 percent of the eligible voters had voted in 1964, and it allowed the government to send in federal registrars wherever twenty or more valid cases of discrimination were unveiled.

The states affected most were Alabama, Georgia, Louisiana, Mississippi, South Carolina, Virginia, and North Carolina. Federal registrars were sent to thirty-two counties in Alabama, Mississippi, Louisiana, and South Carolina. Within six months 8,000 blacks were added to the voting rolls there, and 250,000 were added nationwide. Nevertheless, because of a manpower shortage, fewer than 50 percent of the counties that needed federal registrars received them. Progress was slow, but it was being made for the first time since Reconstruction.

To protest restrictions against black voters, Martin Luther King, Jr., led a historic march from Selma, Alabama, to the state capital of Montgomery in 1965. The march resulted in passage of the Voting Rights Act of 1965.

Then in the 1970s and 1980s, due to several voter registration drives, blacks began to register and vote in such great numbers that in 1984 the *New York Times* said, "For sweep, breadth and passion, nothing like today's surge of black registration has been experienced recently in American politics. . . . Figures can give only a gross outline of its potential . . . in 1966, 4.4 million [blacks] voted; by 1980, 8 million." In the two-year period from 1980 to 1982 more than one million more blacks registered to vote; 7,000,000 were eligible.

With the increasing number of black voters came an increasing number of black elected officials. Today there are more than 5,400 elected black officials. Of this number 240 are mayors including heads of several major cities—Tom Bradley (Los Angeles), Coleman Young (Detroit) and Harold Washington (Chicago)—and 350 are black state legislators. On the federal level black gains are less impressive. In 1950 there were two black members of the House of Representatives; in 1960, four; in 1972, twelve; and in 1982, nineteen. In an article in *New York* magazine Rev. Jesse Jackson pointed out that in the Deep South, where 42 percent of blacks live, there were only two black congressmen out of 132 in 1980. He also said, "Only 1% of the American public officials are black, but we're 12% of the population. We're 46,000 short of our share." Rev. Jackson's campaign for the Democratic presidential nomination in 1984 made political history by putting pressure on the Democrats to take black interests into account in writing party policies.

The real importance of the vote for blacks is not told in numbers, however. Its importance is that it changed the way millions of blacks live; with the vote, blacks won many other rights, and ended many abuses against them. As black militant leader Stokely Carmichael wrote in 1969, "If a Negro is elected sheriff, he can end police brutality. If a black man is elected tax assessor, he can collect and channel funds for the building of better roads and schools serving black people—thus advancing the move from political power into economic areas."

The vote was a step toward ending discrimination against blacks.

5

Women Fight for the Vote

Resolved:
That it is the duty of women of this country to secure to themselves their sacred right of the elective franchise.

Declaration of Sentiments and Resolutions, 1848

The woman suffrage movement is usually dated from July 1848 when a group of women met in Seneca Falls, New York, and issued their Declaration of Sentiments and Resolutions, an eleven-point document outlining their demands for equal rights. All of the resolutions (including property ownership) were passed unanimously except the one demanding the vote, which passed only over the opposition of some delegates. Some of the women thought it would make them look "ridiculous" because at the time it was widely believed that women were both physically and mentally inferior to men and therefore should not have the right to vote.

When the declaration was issued, single women usually lived at home under the rules of their fathers; married women lived under the "rule" of their husbands. Lucretia Coffin Mott, a suffragist, or supporter of female suffrage, said, "Man and woman were created equals, but . . . man has made a civic corpse of the married woman." By law married women were not allowed to own property even if they had inherited it; they were unable to sign contracts or to sue; they were unable to retain custody of their children; even their clothes and wages belonged to their husbands. It was legal for husbands to beat their wives "moderately"— according to one court ruling, with a stick no thicker than a man's thumb. Naturally, women were not allowed to serve on juries or to vote.

The Seneca Falls Convention, the first of hundreds of women's conventions, was the result of the efforts of Lucretia Mott and Elizabeth Cady Stanton. Both had been active in the antislavery movement. When they were rejected as delegates to an abolitionist convention in Great Britain because of their sex, they vowed to turn their attention to women's rights. Both were wives and mothers, but they devoted a considerable amount of time and energy to the women's cause, especially Stanton.

Hundreds of people, especially women who worked, attended the convention in Seneca Falls, traveling by foot and horse and buggy to get there. Many, mostly men, went to jeer. The event received considerable press attention, most of it negative. Given the climate of the times, cartoonists found the declaration an easy target for humor and satire; one headline read "Insurrection Among Women."

Like P. T. Barnum, the famous circus owner who believed that all publicity was good publicity, Stanton welcomed the coverage. She said, "It might start women thinking, and men, too; when men and women think about a new question the first step in progress is taken."

The third woman who was to devote her life to women's causes was Susan B. Anthony, who was told about the convention by her father. As a Quaker, she had shunned politics because the government supported war—a position that violated the Quakers' pacifist beliefs. Initially, Anthony was not very interested in the vote; her principal crusades were against alcohol and for property rights for women. However, she quickly learned that women were not taken seriously because they lacked political power. Once she realized that women needed the vote in order to achieve anything, she worked unceasingly to get it.

Anthony and Stanton met in Rochester, New York, following an antislavery meeting, and although they were not alike—Anthony was more serious and a tireless worker—they forged a friendship that lasted a lifetime, despite serious disagreements along the way. Like many of the early suffragists, Stanton and Anthony cut their teeth on the movements against alcohol and slav-

*Susan B. Anthony and
Elizabeth Cady Stanton
pioneered the fight
for women's suffrage.*

ery, learning to write speeches, raise money, and speak in public—all shocking things for women to do.

Another suffragist who emerged from the abolition movement was Lucy Stone. She began to incorporate comments on the equal rights of women into her antislavery speeches in the 1840s and was severely criticized for it. Stone replied coolly, "I was a woman before I was an abolitionist."

In October, 1850, Stone organized a National Woman's Rights Convention in Worcester, Massachusetts. There it was resolved that "women are clearly entitled to the right of suffrage" and that "the word *male* should be stricken from every state constitution." Over 1,000 people attended the convention, including the black leader and former slave Frederick Douglass. (An early advocate of female suffrage, he later withdrew his support, saying black rights were the first priority.)

Throughout the 1850s women's rights conventions took place everywhere and soon established themselves as an annual ritual. Among these, one stands out—the Akron, Ohio, Convention of 1851. It was there that the famous black suffragist Sojourner Truth gave her speech, "Ain't I a Woman," a classic testament that was almost not given. There were objections to her presence on the platform, and one woman said, "It will ruin us. Every newspaper in the land will have our cause mixed up with abolition and niggers and we shall be denounced."

Frances Gage, the chairperson, was forceful and insisted that Sojourner Truth be given her chance to speak. And she spoke brilliantly. Dismissing the male myth that women are the weaker sex, she told the audience, "I have ploughed, and planted and gathered into barns, and no man could head me. And ain't I a woman? I could work as much and eat as much as a man—when

I could get it—and bear the lash as well! And ain't I a woman?" She sat down amidst wild cheering and applause.

What women wanted were equal rights in everything, especially economic matters. During the 1850s Anthony spent most of her time obtaining signatures on petitions asking legislators to pass a law allowing married women to own property. She traveled all over the state, often on foot; she endured sour food, lumpy mattresses, and frostbite in order to obtain 10,000 signatures.

Despite her amazing efforts, Susan B. Anthony was treated with scorn by legislators. They told her, "Ladies always have the best place and the choicest tidbits at the table. They have the best seat in the [railroad] cars, carriages, and sleighs; the warmest place in winter, and the coolest place in summer. It has thus appeared to the married gentlemen of your Committee, that if there is any inequality or oppression in your case, the gentlemen are the sufferers."

What Anthony saw was far different. In a letter to Stanton she wrote, "As I passed from town to town, I was made to feel the evil of woman's utter dependence on men. . . . There is no true freedom for women without possession of equal property rights and these can be obtained only through legislation." Her experience made her realize even more fully the need for women to get the vote, and thus the right to elect and influence legislators.

More determined than ever, she stepped up her efforts to obtain property and voting rights for women. In 1860 New York State finally gave women the right to control property they had inherited, and their own earnings and joint custody of their children. This reform was short-lived: Two years later, in the midst of the Civil War, New York amended the law to make it completely ineffective.

The women's rights issue was all but forgotten during the Civil War. Conventions came to an end, and women worked primarily to help blacks. The one positive aspect of the war for women was that since men were needed as soldiers, doors were opened for them to fill jobs in such areas as typesetting and nursing, which had previously been closed to them.

The suffragists fully expected to get the vote if the blacks got it, and they worked hard for the cause. However, the women's movement suffered a serious setback when many abolitionists refused to link black suffrage with the women's cause. Horace Greeley told Anthony, "This is a critical period for the Republican party and the life of the Nation. It would be wise and magnanimous of you to hold your claims in abeyance until the Negro is safe beyond peradventure, and your turn will come next."

Anthony felt betrayed by the abolitionists. Wendell Phillips believed combining the two movements would "lose for the Negro more than we should gain for the women." But Sojourner Truth advised Anthony to work for female suffrage "while things are stirring: because if we wait till it is still, it will take a great while to get it going again."

Anthony and the other suffragists worked hard to lobby for the women's vote; the cooperation between the blacks and the suffragists ended unhappily. Stanton and Anthony abandoned the Equal Rights Association, which had worked for the rights of both blacks and women, and formed the National Woman Suffrage Association (NWSA).

Horace Greeley, once an ally of the women suffragists, became their enemy. Sarcastically he asked Anthony, "Are you aware that the bullet and the ballot go together. If you vote are you also prepared to fight?"

Referring to Greeley's work as a journalist and editor, Anthony calmly replied, "Certainly, Mr. Greeley. Just as you fought in the late war—at the point of a goose and quill."

Despite the suffragists' efforts, Congress passed the Fifteenth Amendment giving the vote to blacks only. The suffragists were extremely bitter and angry. Said Julia Ward Howe, "For the first time, we saw . . . every Negro man governing every white woman. This seemed to me intolerable tyranny."

The suffragists then turned their efforts to obtaining the vote for women state by state, and to working against the ratification of the Fifteenth Amendment. When Kansas put a referendum, or open vote, on the ballot asking the voters to decide whether or not to extend the franchise to blacks and women, suffragists including Anthony poured into the state; they spoke, they marched, and they handed out pamphlets door to door. Out of the 30,000 votes cast, about 10,000 said yes to black suffrage; 9,000 to women's. Again the women were angry over their defeat, but determined to continue the fight.

While she was campaigning in Kansas, Anthony met George Francis Train, a wealthy eccentric who supported the woman suffrage movement. He offered her the money to launch a suffrage newspaper. In return, he wanted to write a column about economics in the paper. Since Anthony was very concerned about the plight of the average working woman, she agreed despite his unsavory reputation. Thus, the *Revolution*, which he named, was born. Its motto was "Men, their rights and nothing more; women, their rights, and nothing less."

Because of Train's highly controversial economic theories and opinions, and Anthony's denunciations of the Fifteenth Amendment, she lost more former friends. William Lloyd Garrison, a leading abolitionist, told her, "I regret . . . that you and Mrs. Stanton should have taken such leave of good sense as to be traveling companions and associate lecturers with that crack-brained harlequin and semi-lunatic, George Francis Train. . . . He may be of use in drawing an audience, but so would be a kangaroo, a gorilla, or a hippopotamus."

The suffrage movement suffered losses from the ranks of women as well, for Anthony and Stanton were extraordinarily liberal and they openly advocated divorce from drunken men, and birth control. That was enough to make more modest women blush. But they went further. They gave their support to Victoria Woodhull, a flamboyant, scandalous woman who matched Train in eccentricity. She said it was her "inalienable right" to have as many lovers as she wanted, and she ran for the presidency because she claimed she had been told in a vision that she was destined to win.

Lucy Stone and the more conservative suffragists broke away from Anthony's National Woman Suffrage Association and founded the American Woman Suffrage Association (AWSA). The AWSA began to publish its own noncontroversial newspaper, the *Woman's Journal*. Since the women's movement was not large enough to adequately support two, that was the death blow for the *Revolution* (which had been foundering financially).

For twenty years the two organizations, the NWSA and the AWSA, went their separate ways. The NWSA attracted the younger more radical and more enterprising women, and they worked for a constitutional amendment to get the vote. The AWSA directed its efforts towards getting the states to give women the vote, a tactic Anthony believed would take too long.

In the meantime Anthony tried to get the courts to declare that voting is the right of all citizens. Based on the fact that the Fourteenth Amendment had made women citizens, in 1872 she went to the polls and over the objections of the voting registrar she cast her ballot for the presidency. Two weeks later she was arrested for voting illegally, and she made the most of the occasion by delivering a new speech, "Is It a Crime for a United States Citizen to Vote?" She, of course, did not think so, and many attorneys agreed with her. But the judge in her case, Associate Justice Ward Hunt, was not among them. In a highly unusual move, Hunt dismissed the jurors—some of whom later said they agreed with Anthony—and found her guilty. He fined her $100 plus court costs, but she refused to pay the fine. Ordinarily she would have been jailed, but she wasn't, possibly to keep her from entering an appeal and bringing the case to the Supreme Court. But another woman did.

Like Anthony, Virginia Minor, her friend and president of the Missouri Woman Suffrage Association, tried to vote in 1872. But the election registrar refused to let her. She brought suit against him, claiming he interfered with her right to vote as a citizen. She argued her case all the way to the Supreme Court, but in *Minor* v. *Happersett* the Court ruled that the Constitution "does not confer the right of suffrage upon anyone, and that the constitutions and laws of the several states which commit that important trust to men alone are not necessarily void." That decision was a devastating blow to women and later to blacks, because it was used as a precedent to argue that the states had the right to establish voter restrictions that effectively disenfranchised blacks as well as women.

Following the decision, it was clear that to avoid fighting for the right to vote state by state—a time-consuming, tedious process—women needed a constitutional amendment. In 1878 Senator Aaron Sargent of California finally introduced the proposed Sixteenth Amendment, referred to as the Anthony Amendment. It said simply, "The right of citizens of the United States to vote shall not be denied or abridged by the United States or any state on account of sex." For forty-two years the Amendment remained unchanged—and unpassed although both the House and Senate committees favored it in 1882.

In addition to the argument that it was a state's right to establish who votes, there were many other arguments against female suffrage. Some opponents declared it would destroy homes and break up families; others argued that the vote would degrade women. Said Senator George C. Vest in 1887, "It would take her down from that pedestal where she is today, influencing by her gentle and kindly caress the action of her husband towards the good and the pure."

Anthony saw women's role in society for what it was: second class. She maintained, "Disfranchisement says to all women: 'Your judgment is not sound; your opinions are not worthy of being counted.' Man is the superior, woman the subject, under the present condition of political affairs, and until this great wrong is righted, ignorant men and small boys will continue to look with disdain on the opinion of women."

Meanwhile, none of the dire consequences predicted by the antisuffragists had occurred in the few states where women voted. In 1869 the Wyoming ter-

These women in Cheyenne, Wyoming Territory, were the first to vote in the United States.

ritory had adopted a constitution that granted universal suffrage to men and women. When Wyoming asked to join the Union, Congress put pressure on it to disenfranchise women, but the western legislators held firm. They even adopted the motto, "America will be a better place to live when women go to the polls." That was one obvious reason the women had been granted the ballot—to help tame the near-lawlessness of Wyoming.

Until after the turn of the century, however, only a handful of states, all western, gave women the right to vote. One reason the West acted before the East was that women had been accepted and treated as equals in the Granges, the farmers' organizations that were vital in pressuring Congress to protect agricultural interests. In 1893 Colorado became the second state to enfranchise women, thanks in large part to the work of Carrie Chapman Catt, who succeeded Anthony as the leading suffragist. By then the two suffrage organizations had merged into the National American Woman Suffrage Association (NAWSA).

On her eightieth birthday in 1900, Anthony was given a jeweled pin of the American flag; each state where women were allowed to vote was represented by a diamond; there were four. Indiana and Utah, in an effort by the Mormans to retain control over the new settlers moving into that state, had given women the vote in 1896. Those victories were small consolation for the defeat of the Anthony Amendment, which had been introduced into Congress every year since 1887 and had been bottled up in committee every year.

As her life drew to an end Anthony wrote to Stanton, "It is fifty-one years since we first met. . . . We little dreamed . . . that half a century later we would be compelled to leave the finish of the battle to another generation of women. But . . . there is an army of them where we were but a handful."

At her last convention in 1906, after a lifetime of fighting for suffrage, Susan B. Anthony said, "The fight must not cease; you must see that it does not stop." Her last words in public were: "Failure is impossible."

6

Women Triumph

When women shall have become used to politics, we shall find that we have harnessed an unruly Niagara. They will subdue politics to their hearts' desire, change it as men would never dream of changing it, wreck it savagely in the face of our masculine protest and merrily rebuild it anew in the face of our despair.

Floyd Dell, 1913

Before her death in 1906, Anthony had turned over the reins of the National American Woman Suffrage Association to Carrie Chapman Catt, telling the group simply, "I present to you my successor."

Catt, a college graduate and former teacher, brought her own style to NAWSA and got as much publicity and support as possible. She once said, "Never again will suffrage cease to be front-page news." At conventions, she organized workshops on such topics as "How to Get Press Coverage" and "How to Work with Labor."

Catt worked to get labor unions to support female suffrage by capitalizing on the turmoil regarding child-labor laws, or rather the lack of them, and the intolerable working conditions in many factories. These made the news tragically when a fire broke out in the Triangle Shirtwaist factory in New York in 1911. Because they were locked inside and unable to get out, over 100 women perished. Catt succeeded in getting over forty labor unions to back the suffrage movement, including the influential American Federation of Labor (AFL), which was then led by Samuel Gompers.

By 1900 about 5,000,000 women were working, many in jobs once held only by men. But conservatives still considered the woman's place to be "in the home." Like many men, former President Grover Cleveland opposed suffrage for women and in the May 1905 issue of *Ladies' Home Journal,* he wrote, "No sensible man has fears of injury to the country on account of [woman suffrage]. It is its dangerous, undermining effect on the character of the wives and mothers of our land that we fear." He believed that politics, often labeled "dirty" at the time because of voting frauds, would corrupt women. The majority of older women agreed with him.

Carrie Chapman Catt, who succeeded Susan B. Anthony as head of the National American Woman Suffrage Association

*Suffragists rally in support
of women's right to vote.*

The ranks of the suffragists, however, were swelled by the young college women, who had been allowed to attend school because of the efforts of women like Susan B. Anthony. The new generation of suffragists changed the movement and brought more radical attitudes to it. They adopted the motto Into the Streets, and went out demonstrating and singing such songs as "Give the Ballot to the Mothers."

Suffragists began to organize parades as well as conventions. After the first parade in New York in 1910, they marched all over the country, wearing yellow sashes that read, Votes for Women. Such tactics were thought by many to be "shocking," and the suffragists received a lot of attention from the press. Unfortunately, most of it was unfavorable. An editorial in the *New York Times* (May 5, 1912) denounced suffrage and stated that it would harm women: "The ballot will secure to woman no right that she needs and does not now possess. That is a true statement, and we hold that it is not debatable. Woman is thoroughly protected by the existing laws. In her pursuit of all privileges and duties of men, however, she is deliberately endangering many rights she now enjoys without legal sanction. It will be a sad day for society when woman loses the respect she now receives from all but the basest of men." Such thinking totally ignored the many problems of women, including low wages and physical abuse by their husbands.

The myth that women are the "weaker sex" was widespread. A number of unsubstantiated and illogical statements about women were made even by respectable magazines. Editor Edward Bok of the *Ladies' Home Journal*, wrote, "[There is] an alarming tendency among business girls and women to nervous collapse."

Yet it was female opposition and indifference that was the bigger problem. Said Agnes Irwin, once dean of Radcliffe College, "The active participation of women in politics would be a great and perhaps hazardous experiment in government. I am opposed to trying it." Mrs. Benjamin Harrison, wife of the former president, said, "I cannot interest myself in the subject in the slightest degree."

Many men and women joined the Anti-Suffrage Association, and the suffragists suffered many defeats as several states refused to extend the vote to women. Among the few states that did allow women to vote were Washington, in 1910; California, in 1911; and Kansas, Arizona, and Oregon, in 1912. The first state east of the Mississippi River to give women the vote was Illinois, in 1913. Elsewhere women won limited voting rights; in Louisiana they were allowed to vote in local referendums; in Massachusetts, for school board members. Those were matters said to be best handled by women because of their "natural" interest in the home and education.

On the national level, however, women were making no progress. In the election of 1912 the Republican candidate, William Howard Taft, opposed woman suffrage. Woodrow Wilson, the Democratic Candidate, favored state-by-state suffrage for women instead of a national amendment. Only the third-party Populist candidate, former Republican Teddy Roosevelt, endorsed the Anthony Amendment in his effort to get the women's vote in the suffrage states. The NAWSA, which had always been nonpartisan, refused to back Roosevelt, but many state chapters worked hard for him. Wilson, however, won the election.

Once in the White House, Wilson changed his mind and eventually endorsed the Anthony Amendment after a dramatic turn in the suffrage movement. It became more militant, and Wilson got his first taste of it the day before his inauguration.

Two young NAWSA members, Alice Paul and Lucy Burns, organized a massive march in Washington, D. C. In what the *New York Times* called an "astonishing demonstration," over 5,000 men and women paraded in support of women suffrage; about 500,000 people lined the streets to watch. Some of the spectators tripped, slapped, spat on, or burned the marchers with cigars as the police stood by and did nothing. Federal troops were called out to control the crowd and the event made national headlines.

Both Paul and Burns had taken part in the suffrage movement in Great Britain, which had been led by Emmeline Pankhurst—infamous for throwing bricks through the windows of Parliament to dramatize women's anger at being denied the vote. Both Paul and Burns had come to believe that such bold tactics were necessary in the United States.

Catt and other leaders of the NAWSA disagreed with them, and they were asked to refrain from militant tactics or drop out of the organization. They withdrew and began their own organization, the Congressional Union. The CU, besides organizing fund-raising drives and circulating petitions, put on publicity stunts such as car races and stole the front page headlines from the NAWSA for the next several years. Once again the suffragists were divided, but the NAWSA, the radical group in the 1870s, was now the conservative one.

Then the CU, later known as the National Women's Party (NWP), took a step that the NAWSA denounced as foolish. Since both the Senate and the House of Representatives were controlled by the Democrats, the CU decided to hold the Democrats responsible for the failure of Congress to pass the Anthony Amendment; the group worked to defeat all the Democratic candidates in the 1914 election. The CU was very effective, and due in part to their efforts twenty-three out of forty Democrats lost their bids for office. Ironically, while this demonstrated the potential power of the women's vote, all twenty-three were suffrage supporters.

The suffrage issue was placed on a back burner in the presidential race of 1916. World War I was raging in Europe, and Wilson campaigned with the slogan, He Kept Us Out of War. It helped him defeat Republican Charles Evan Hughes, a supporter of female suffrage, but within months of the election Wilson asked Congress to declare war. In April 1917 the United States entered the war, in Wilson's words, "to make the world safe for democracy."

The Civil War had brought the suffrage movement for women to a standstill, but the new suffragists were not willing to sit out World War I. They continued to pressure Congress, and they picketed the White House with signs reading, Democracy Begins at Home. At first the "sentinels of liberty," which is what the NWP called its demonstrators, carried on without problems. But within six months they began to be harassed by many, especially soldiers and sailors, for not supporting the war effort.

Suffragist Ernestine Hara Kettler was a sentinel. She later recalled, "There were always men and women standing there harassing us and throwing pretty bad insults—and pretty obscene ones. The women weren't obscene, but the men were. Our instructions were to pay absolutely no attention to them. I ignored them. I was brave. My goodness, I was fighting for a cause."

Soon the women were subjected to more violent abuse. They were pelted with tomatoes and rotten eggs; smoke was blown into their faces. To put an end to the unpleasant incidents, the police arrested not the spectators who were violent but the women on the picket line. They were charged with obstructing traffic, found guilty by the hundreds, and fined. Like Anthony before them, many refused to pay their fines; unlike Anthony, they were sent to jail, some for as long as six months.

The suffragists were treated like hard-core criminals, sometimes worse. Kettler said, "The food was the greatest problem we had. It was just unbelievable—the worms that were found in the oatmeal, in the soup we ate." She went on, "We all suffered. This was before the hunger strikes, but some of the women were actually on a hunger strike already. They just couldn't eat. The only thing they could eat was bread, if it wasn't totally moldy and if it didn't show rat tracks."

Because of the inedible food, the women later waged hunger strikes. Many of them were then force-fed by having tubes shoved down their throats and into their stomachs. Said Kettler, "They received very severe treatment. They were beaten and dragged across the patio from the superintendent's office to their cells. Some women had broken ribs and were bleeding profusely and they weren't treated. Others had all kinds of lacerations."

Word of the women's treatment soon reached the press, and the public was outraged—including President Wilson, who ordered their release from prison. They were also exonerated by the court, which ruled they had been arrested and tried illegally.

Simultaneously other women were showing the capabilities of the "weaker sex" by toiling in aircraft and munitions factories, driving ambulances, nursing the wounded, and taking over wherever they were needed to replace men who were fighting in Europe. Thousands more women enlisted in the military. Secretary of War Newton D. Baker said, "[What] this war is bringing home to us is that men and women are essentially partners in an industrial civilization. . . ."

Within that climate Wilson changed his mind about women's suffrage, and he personally asked Congress to grant it. Emotions for and against it ran so high that ailing Representative Harry Barnhard had himself carried into the House on a stretcher in order to vote Yea. His heroic effort helped the Amendment pass the House by a vote of 274–136, exactly the two-thirds needed to pass a constitutional amendment.

But the Senate defeated it. Some senators believed it was a states' rights issue, and many others strongly believed that the vote for women would be disastrous. The prestigious *New York Times* ran the following editorial on February 2, 1917: "That the female mind is inferior to the male mind need not be assumed; that there is something about it essentially different, and that this difference is of a kind and degree that with votes for women would constitute a political danger is or ought to be plain to everybody."

Such thinking, though it is hard to believe now, was not uncommon. Nevertheless, Wilson, whose daughter was a suffragist, went to the Senate to plead for the Anthony Amendment. He said, "We have made partners of the women in this war; shall we admit them only to a partnership of sacrifice and suffering and toil, and not to a partnership of privilege and right?" Despite his plea, the Senate defeated the amendment by two votes; it was defeated again in February 1919, by one vote.

In the interim Michigan, South Dakota, Oklahoma, Ohio, Indiana, Nebraska, New York, Montana, and Nevada had enfranchised women, bringing the total number of suffrage states to fifteen out of forty-five. New Jersey, Wilson's home state, Pennsylvania, and Massachusetts had voted against female suffrage.

Then, unexpectedly, the Senate passed the amendment on June 4, 1919, and sent it to the states for ratification.

The suffragists' happiness was short-lived, however, for very few of the state legislatures were in session and most of them met every other year, on the odd year. That meant the majority were scheduled to meet a year after the next presidential election in 1920. Given their long struggle to win the vote, the suffragists were running out of patience. They wanted to vote in 1920!

The one hope, Catt saw, was for the governors to call special sessions. But special sessions were both expensive and unpopular, so it was necessary for Catt and others to cajole, plead, and pressure them. Catt told them that women would remember their friends when they got the vote, which was now viewed as inevitable and just a question of time. (The same tactic was later adopted by the National Organization of Women, or NOW, which uses as one of its slogans, We'll Remember Each November.

Many governors called special sessions, and within a year thirty-five states had ratified the Nineteenth Amendment, which had first been proposed as the Sixteenth. One more state was needed for it to become law, and during the summer of 1920 it was introduced on the floor of Tennessee's legislative house.

Catt went to Tennessee and used every trick she knew to get votes for the amendment, but up to the last minute its future was in doubt. The vote was a cliffhanger. The final vote in favor was cast by a twenty-four-year-old legislator who said, "A mother's advice is always safest for her boy to follow and my mother wanted me to vote for ratification." Tennessee ratified the Nineteenth Amendment on August 18, 1920, and eight days later it was signed into law by Wilson. It read, as it had always read, "The right of citizens of the United States to vote shall not be denied or abridged by the United States or by any State on account of sex."

It had taken women almost a century to win the vote, and Catt told those who had sat on the sidelines, "Women have suffered an agony of soul which you can never comprehend that you and your daughters might inherit political freedom. That vote has been costly. Prize it!"

Almost everyone expected women to change politics, but they didn't; the "woman's vote" never materialized. Initially only about 35 percent of the eligible women even voted, because many of them believed it was not "ladylike." Many others stayed home because their husbands objected to women voting, especially since voting often took place in the back rooms of saloons. Not until 1936 did more than 50 percent of the eligible women vote, and by then it was clear that women, like men, had diverse views on national policies and had not formed a bloc. In fact, one observer at the time noted that nothing had changed in politics except that married men now had two votes, for husbands and wives nearly always voted for the same candidates.

The biggest failure of women, however, was that too few of them understood how the political system worked, and did not build networks or power bases. In a 1973 interview suffragist Laura Ellsworth Seiler recalled, "At the time I think it hadn't occurred to a great many women once they got the vote, the rest wouldn't be easy. I think most men felt that. I remember once, when watching the polls, I was talking to a Tammany boss [political leaders in New York who controlled the vote through fraud and corruption] who was also watching. He said, 'Of course, I'm opposed to woman's suffrage. Once women get the vote, they can get practically everything they want.' That was more or less the attitude. It didn't occur to them that women's groups were going to break up as soon as the vote was won. They let their organizations go and most of them paid no further attention."

Suffragist Florence Kiltchelt agreed with Seiler. "After we got the vote, the crusade was over. It was peacetime and we went back to a hundred different causes and tasks that we'd been putting off all those years."

The next women's cause—the Equal Rights Amendment—was even more controversial than the vote, and many suffragists were against it themselves. First introduced in 1923, the ERA said, and still does, "Equality of rights under the law shall not be denied or abridged by the United States or by any State on account of sex."

At the time labor unions opposed the ERA because they had fought to get legislation protecting female workers from a number of flagrant abuses at work, such as lifting heavy loads while pregnant. They believed that equal rights for women would undo their efforts; however, Alice Paul believed that such laws would work against women in the future. She was proved correct, and women were relegated to "pink ghetto" jobs like typing, which paid very little in comparison to men's salaries.

Beside the controversy over the ERA, women were

unable to become an integral part of the political system because they were given the "dirty jobs": selling tickets to fund-raising dinners, mailing election brochures, giving teas, and driving voters to the polls. They were not given positions within the two major parties and did not gain a voice in making policies and platform positions. By 1924 Emily Newell Blair, a Democratic committee woman, said, "I know of no politician who is afraid of the women's vote on any question under the sun." Women were still politically powerless.

In the 1940s, as they had done many times before, women rallied around men and supported them during World War II. They went back to the factories to produce war supplies. The era was symbolized by Rosie the Riveter, a woman who replaced a man in a "man's job."

Yet a February 1943 editorial in the *Woman's Home Companion* read: "I have attained Cabinet rank [President Roosevelt had appointed Frances Perkins secretary of labor], I have won business position. I have become a great writer and painter and a glorious voice. I have brought mercy to the fighting front, I have ferried bombers, I have taken my place in factories at machines. But still I remain a woman—to be regarded as a woman, excused as a woman, paid as a woman."

The women's movement of the 1940s died almost as soon as the war ended. Sociologist David Riesman wrote in 1949, "There is an increasing submissiveness of women to what men want of them and to the world as man has largely made it."

During the 1950s and 1960s women made almost no impact on politics. The handful of women who served in Congress were generally appointed to fill the unexpired terms of their husbands who had died in office. Rarely did any of them, with the notable exception of

Senator Margaret Chase Smith of Maine, go on to win office on their own. Although Smith served on a number of important Senate committees and was nominated for the presidency in 1964, she was best known for wearing a red rose on her lapel every day; her press coverage was generally relegated to the women's pages.

Overall the history of women in Congress has been dismal. Out of 10,000 members of both the Senate and the House of Representatives, only about 100 have been women. Thanks to the women's movement during the 1970s, women began to make some progress, particularly on the local and state levels. Still, only 13 percent of the state legislators were women in 1983, and only 24, or about 5 percent, of the total 535 members of Congress were women.

A major problem for women is the high cost of running for office. Nancy Stevenson, former lieutenant governor of South Carolina, said in 1983, "I think women always have more difficulty raising money because they are generally perceived as unlikely to win. We're not part of the 'old boy' network, which is apt to rally around one of its own."

Political history was made, however, when the Democratic party nominated Geraldine Ferraro as Walter F. Mondale's vice presidential running mate in the 1984 election against incumbent Ronald Reagan. For the first time since its founding in 1968, the National Organization for Women (NOW), endorsed a candidate, Walter Mondale, primarily because Reagan opposed abortion and the ERA.

Nevertheless, the Democrats failed to attract the wide support from women they expected. About 57 percent of the women who voted cast their ballots for Reagan. The economy proved to be the overriding issue and there was a widespread feeling that Reagan had

Geraldine Ferraro, shown here with Walter Mondale at the 1984 Democratic Convention, made history when she accepted her party's nomination as the first woman candidate for vice-president of the United States.

reduced inflation and had improved the economy. Most voters opposed Mondale's plan to raise taxes.

What Ferraro's candidacy did gain for women was more activism. As Kathy Wilson, the co-chairperson of the National Women's Political Caucus, said, women's progress in politics is, as in the past, "measured in inches, not miles."

7 The Young Voter

You are coming to maturity
at a time which history
will remember as a great period
of emancipation for young
Americans. Your generation has
the opportunity to participate
more fully in the American
adventure than young people
have ever been able to do since
Revolutionary times 200 years ago.

Richard M. Nixon, 1971

When the Twenty-Sixth Amendment to the Constitution was ratified in 1971 and eighteen-to-twenty-one-year-olds were given the right to vote, it ended a centuries-old tradition that twenty-one was the "right" age to vote. That tradition was based on a variety of reasons attributed to superstition, religious belief, and even to the fact that in England during the Middle Ages the armor the knights wore was so heavy that the king set twenty-one as the age when boys would be strong enough to carry it, and thus to fight.

Whatever the reason, twenty-one was established as the voting age in England when the colonists first came to the New World, and soon it was established in the colonies as well. For a very short time during the mid-1600s, Virginia taxed every man sixteen years of age or older and also gave them the right to vote, but that practice ended by the end of the century.

Age restrictions were sometimes vague; for instance, New Jersey gave the vote to those of "full maturity." But it was generally understood that only those over twenty-one could vote, and when the states rewrote their constitutions in the late 1700s and early 1800s, they specified twenty-one as the minimum age for voting. During the Revolutionary War there had been complaints among the young soldiers that they were not allowed to vote, but at the time there were many other restrictions on suffrage, and their dissatisfaction was ignored.

Throughout our history young men have argued that the right to vote should go hand in hand with military duty. During the Civil War boys as young as fourteen fought on both sides, and there was widespread sentiment among them that they had earned the right to vote. The issue was debated by state legislators in several states including New York, where Marcus Bicford argued, "In this age in which we live, in this fast age, men mature both in body and in mind at a great deal earlier period than formerly." His argument was not successful, however, and the age was not lowered. The same argument was advanced often during the next 100 years, always with the same results.

The question of lowering the voting age was not a hot issue again until young men and women went to the front during World War I to serve as soldiers or medics. They argued, "Old enough to fight, old enough to vote," but once again the age was not lowered, and after the war the issue withered.

Before the outbreak of World War II, 79 percent of the people who responded to a Gallup poll were against lowering the voting age. Once war broke out, however, public attitudes changed dramatically, and 58 percent of the people were in favor of changing the voting age to eighteen as there were 200,000 men and women between the ages of eighteen and twenty-one in the military. As Clarence Linton, professor of education at Columbia University said, "It is youth, more than any other age group, who make the sacrifices, in blood, sweat, tears and lost opportunities."

President Franklin D. Roosevelt told the young soldiers, "We know that wisdom does not come necessarily with years, that old men may be foolish and young men wise." Yet he did not ask Congress to enfranchise the eighteen-to-twenty-one-year-olds, and did not support the resolution for an amendment to lower the age to eighteen that Jennings Randolph of West Virginia introduced in the House of Representatives in 1942.

Many arguments pro and con were heard about the resolution to amend the Constitution. W. R. McCarthy, the national secretary-treasurer during the war, believed that "[if you] give youth a chance it will prove that it fights democracy's battles as well with ballots as it does with bullets." The National Education Association also endorsed lowering the voting age: "The youth who have just finished high school are among our most thoroughly informed citizens. They are well equipped to assume this new responsibility."

Others argued that the young were not well informed—that they would fall under the spell of political villains and become like the Hitler youth, young people who were organized into groups and taught to inform the military about "enemies" of the Third Reich. Some of them turned in their parents or neighbors for hiding Jews.

The major opposition to lowering the voting age came from Southern Democrats who opposed a constitutional amendment because it would infringe on the states' rights to establish their own voting qualifications and would destroy their methods of keeping blacks out of the voting booth. They blocked the bill, and after the war interest in it faded.

During the Korean War the issue predictably came back to life. President Dwight D. Eisenhower asked Congress to lower the voting age, but again the Southern Democrats wielded enough power to kill the amendment. Although his own state had lowered the voting age to eighteen, Georgia's Senator Richard Russell led the fight against it, arguing again that it was a states' right. When the Senate voted on the amendment, thirty-four were in favor and twenty-four against, five votes short of the necessary two-thirds needed to amend the Constitution.

In the meantime several state legislatures had debated the issue, but only Georgia and Kentucky (1955) lowered the voting age to eighteen; Hawaii, which became a state in 1959, came into the Union with a voting age of twenty, and Alaska came in with a minimum age of nineteen.

On the national level the issue was brought to the forefront again by the Vietnam War in the 1960s. But this time there was a major difference; the decade was dominated by the young, who were politically very active. They protested the Vietnam War, demonstrated for civil rights, and demanded clean air and water. Given this atmosphere, the time was right for Congress to reconsider lowering the voting age. A report prepared for President Lyndon B. Johnson stated, "lowering the voting age will not eliminate protest by the young. But it will provide them with a direct, constructive and democratic channel for making their views felt and for giving them a reasonable stake in the future of the nation."

Nevertheless, the Southern Democrats continued to oppose an amendment to the Constitution even though the Supreme Court had either weakened or eliminated ploys to keep blacks out of the voting booth. Through new laws Congress had also eroded many of the state qualifications that had been devised to discriminate against some voters.

Because of the opposition to an amendment lowering the voting age, Senator Mike Mansfield of Montana tried a new tactic. He added a rider, or section, that gave eighteen-to-twenty-one-year-olds the vote to the Voting Rights Act of 1970. Essentially the Voting Rights Act extended the Voting Rights Act of 1965, which had been passed to protect black voting rights. The bill, which needed only a majority vote in favor, was passed and sent to President Richard M. Nixon. The bill needed his signature to go into effect, but Nixon publicly wondered whether or not it was constitutional; he believed it interfered with the states' rights to establish voter qualifications. He hesitated but finally signed it. He stated that "the reason the voting age should be lowered is not that 18 year olds are old enough to fight. It is because they are smart enough to vote. Youth today is not as young as it used to be."

As Nixon and others had expected, the bill was challenged by several states, and the case was brought before the Supreme Court. By a vote of 5–4, the justices ruled that the bill was constitutional, but that it only applied to national elections and that the states still had the right to set the age for their own elections. Justice Black wrote, "It is a plain fact of history that the Framers [of the Constitution] never imagined that the national Congress would set the qualifications for voters in every election from President to local constable or village alderman. It is obvious that the whole Constitution reserves to the States the power to set voter qualifications in state and local elections except to the limited extent that the people through constitutional amendments have specifically narrowed the power of the States."

The Court's ruling unleashed pandemonium. The states were faced with two choices. The first one was to maintain two sets of voting records, one for federal elections in which the eighteen-to-twenty-one-year-olds were now entitled to vote and one for the state or local elections for which they were allowed to set their own age requirement. Two sets of registration records would cost extra money and generate paperwork and confusion. The second choice was to lower the voting age to 18 years of age, but to do that many states would have had to re-write their state constitutions, a long and difficult task. What was needed to eliminate the states' problem was a constitutional amendment lowering the

These high school students—many of whom will soon be eligible to vote—demonstrte their interest in the election process by attending a rally during the 1984 presidential campaign.

voting age in all elections to eighteen, so its opponents were now forced to reconsider.

When the proposed Twenty-Sixth Amendment giving the vote to eighteen- to twenty-one-year-olds was introduced in Congress in 1971, it was finally passed. The vote in the House of Representatives was 401 to 19; in the Senate it was 94 to 0. The same day Congress passed the Twenty-Sixth Amendment, Minnesota, Connecticut, Tennessee, and Wisconsin ratified it. Within the record time of three months it was ratified by the necessary thirty-eight states, and on June 30, 1971, it became law.

Because of their deep involvement in the issues of the day, young adults were expected to change the face of politics. In his book *The Party's Over* political analyst David S. Broder wrote, "Historically, young people have registered and voted in far smaller proportions than their elders. But the new generation differs from its predecessors in many respects, and may prove to be more politically active. The young people have significantly more education than their parents—most have at least a high school education, and more than half, some college. Through television, they have been exposed to the world in a way no previous generation has been."

The youth vote, however, never materialized. Of the eleven million eighteen- to twenty-one-year-olds who were enfranchised in 1971, only 50 percent registered to vote by the 1972 presidential election, and of those who had registered about 15 percent failed to show up at the polls.

What happened? Some political analysts said the percentage of young adults who registered was so low because the Republican candidate, Richard M. Nixon, had an overwhelming lead in the polls over Democrat George McGovern, and they saw no reason to vote. Yet in the following elections the registration and turnout among young voters remained about the same.

Many reasons are offered to explain why the young choose not to exercise their right to vote: They do not own property or significant possessions, therefore, they do not have a "stake in society"; they do not have the skills needed to think about the issues; they do not see how voting will personally affect them; because they are more mobile, they must reregister each time they move and many fail to do so; they are interested primarily in personal goals; they often do not join a political party. Whatever the reason, they are growing in numbers, and they are adding to the dismal voting record in the United States. Although voter turnout was up in 1984, reversing a twenty-year trend, only slightly more than half (53 percent) of those eligible voted in the presidential election. In 1960, about 63 percent of those eligible voted; that was the biggest turnout since women were enfranchised in 1920.

Often the eighteen-to-twenty-one year-olds are lumped together with everyone under the age of thirty, but even that larger group has a poor voting record: less than 50 percent of those eligible vote.

Age, of course, is not the only factor that determines whether or not a person votes. Marital status, educational level, and economic level are often reliable indications of who will vote; for example, a person who is married is more likely to vote than one who is single, and the higher the educational level and salary, the more likely a person is to go to the polls.

The high percentage of nonvoters in the United States is troublesome to many political observers because participation by the people is vital to democracy. The vote is a means of changing the goals and the directions of the country to meet the ever-changing attitudes, views, and conditions of the people.

For Further Reading

Alexander, Rae Pace. *Young and Black in America*. New York: Random House, 1970.

Archer, Jules. *Famous Young Rebels*. New York: Messner, 1973.

Bardolph, Richard, ed. *The Civil Rights Record*. New York: Thomas Y. Crowell, 1970.

Bontemps, Arna. *100 Years of Negro Freedom*. New York: Dodd, 1967.

Boynick, David K. *Women Who Led the Way: Eight Pioneers for Equal Rights*. New York: Thomas Y. Crowell, 1972.

Buckmaster, Henrietta. *Women Who Shaped History*. New York: Collier Books, 1966.

Chalmers, David M. *Hooded Americanism: the History of the Ku Klux Klan*. New York: Franklin Watts, 1981.

Cook, Fred J. *The Rise of American Political Parties*. New York: Franklin Watts, 1971.

Dorman, Michael. *Dirty Politics from 1776 to Watergate*. New York: Delacorte Press, 1979.

Findlay, Bruce Allyn. *Your Rugged Constitution*. Stanford, CA.: Stanford University Press, 1969.

Flexner, Eleanor. *Century of Struggle: The Woman's Rights Movement in the United States.* New York: Atheneum, 1971.

Foster, G. Allen. *Votes for Women.* New York: Criterion Books, 1966.

Gurko, Miriam. *The Ladies of Seneca Falls: the Birth of the Woman's Rights Movement.* New York: Schocken, 1976.

Hamilton, Charles. *The Bench and the Ballot.* New York: Oxford University Press, 1973.

Katz, William Loren and Bernard Gaughran. *The Constitutional Amendments.* New York: Franklin Watts, 1974.

King, Martin Luther. *Why We Can't Wait.* New York: Harper, 1958.

Loeb, Robert H. *Your Guide to Voting.* New York: Franklin Watts, 1977.

Lutz, Alma. *Susan B. Anthony.* Boston: Beacon Press, 1960.

O'Donnell, James J. *Every Vote Counts: a Teen-age Guide to the Electoral Process.* New York: Messner, 1976.

O'Neill, William L. *Everyone Was Brave.* Chicago: Quadrangle Press, 1969.

Severn, Bill. *Free But Not Equal: How Women Won the Right to Vote.* New York: Messner, 1967.

Sterne, Emma Gelders. *I Have a Dream.* New York: Knopf, 1965.

Index

Abolitionist movement, 30, 61, 63
Adams, John, 13, 14, 18–19
Age, voting, 90–97
Alabama, 31, 34, 44, 47, 51–53
Alien Act, 19
American Woman Suffrage Association (AWSA), 65
Anthony, Susan B., 59–70, 72
Arkansas, 30, 31, 42, 47

Baker v. *Carr*, 23
Ballots, 39
Black Codes, 30, 32, 33
Black vote, 1, 20, 29–55, 63, 64, 66–67; and civil rights legislation, 49–55; and literacy tests, 26, 42–45, 46, 49; 19th century struggle for, 30–40, 42–43; and poll taxes, 42, 45–47; and white primary, 47–49
Bribes, 2, 8–9
Brown v. *Board of Education of Topeka*, 45, 49–50

California, 26, 76
Carter, Jimmy, 2
Catt, Carrie Chapman, 69, 72, 73, 77, 81, 82
Chute, Marchette, 6
Civil Rights Act (1866), 33
Civil Rights Act (1957), 50
Civil Rights Act (1960), 50–51
Civil War, 30–32, 78, 90
Colonial vote, 5–15, 18
Colorado, 69
Congress, 13–14, 19, 32–33, 36, 47, 52, 78, 84–85, 92–93, 96
Congressional Union (CU), 77–78
Connecticut, 8, 19–20, 26, 30, 36, 42

Constitution, 1, 13–14, 19, 32, 40, 47, 66, 91, 94. *See also* individual amendments

Declaration of Sentiments and Resolutions (1848), 57, 58
Delaware, 24, 30
Democratic party, 18, 39–40, 47–48, 50, 77–78, 92, 93
Depression, 46
Dorr, Thomas, 25–26
Douglass, Frederick, 32, 36, 40, 61
Du Bois, W.E.B., 43

Economic issues, early, 6, 8–15, 23–26
Eisenhower, Dwight D., 92
Election districts, 21, 23
Electoral college, 14, 24
Equal Rights Amendment, 83–84

Federal elections, 14–15
Federalist party, 18–20
Ferraro, Geraldine, 85–87
Fifteenth Amendment, 36, 42, 48, 52, 64
Florida, 31, 34, 39, 46, 51
Fourteenth Amendment, 33, 34, 47, 66
Franklin, Benjamin, 10, 13

Georgia, 12, 30, 31, 34, 52, 92
Gerrymandering, 21, 23
Grandfather clause, 43, 44
Great Britain, 6, 12
Greeley, Horace, 63, 64
Guinn v. *United States*, 44

Hamilton, Alexander, 13, 18
Hayes, Rutherford B., 39–40

House of Representatives, 13–14, 19–20, 40, 80, 85, 96
Howe, Julia Ward, 64

Immigrants, 26, 31, 42
Indiana, 69

Jackson, Andrew, 24–25
Jackson, Jesse, 54
Jefferson, Thomas, 14, 17, 18–19
Jews, 6
Jim Crow laws, 43–44
Johnson, Andrew, 32–33
Johnson, Lyndon B., 52, 93

Kansas, 64, 76
Kennedy, John F., 50
Kennedy, Robert, 50
Kentucky, 31, 36, 92
King, Martin Luther, Jr., 41, 51–52, 53
Korean War, 92
Ku Klux Klan Acts, 37

Lincoln, Abraham, 31, 32
Literacy tests, 26, 42–45, 46, 49
Louisiana, 20, 31, 34, 39, 43, 46, 52, 76

Maine, 26, 30, 31
Manhood suffrage, early 1800s, 20–21
Maryland, 6, 8, 21, 30
Massachusetts, 8, 13, 21, 26, 31, 61, 76, 81
Mayflower Compact, 5, 6, 7
Minor v. Happersett, 66
Mississippi, 20, 31, 34, 42, 45, 46, 47, 52
Mott, Lucretia, 58

National American Woman Suffrage Association (NAWSA), 69, 72, 76, 77

National Association for the Advancement of Colored People (NAACP), 43–44, 49, 51
National Organization of Women (NOW), 81, 85
National Woman Suffrage Association (NWSA), 63, 65
New Hampshire, 12, 31, 45
New Jersey, 10, 81, 90
New York, 6, 9, 20, 23–24, 36, 42, 62–63
Nineteenth Amendment, 81–82
Nixon, Richard, 89, 93–94, 96
North Carolina, 13, 30, 31, 46, 52

Ohio, 20, 36, 61
One man, one vote principle, 23

Paine, Thomas, 8
Penn, William, 10
Pennsylvania, 9, 10, 12, 30, 81
Plessy v. Ferguson, 44–45
Plymouth Colony, 6–8
Political parties: 1800s growth of, 18; and white primary, 47–49. *See also individual parties*
Poll taxes, 42, 45–47
Presidential elections: 1800, 19; 1824, 24; 1876, 39–40; 1916, 78; 1972, 96; 1980, 2; 1984, 2, 85–87, 95, 97
Property rights and restrictions: colonial, 8–15; early 1800s, 20, 25; women's, 62–63

Racism, 37–40, 42–50, 55
Reagan, Ronald, 2, 85
Reconstruction, 32–40
Reconstruction Act of 1867, 33, 35, 37
Registration, voter, 2, 54, 96

Religion, 6
Republican party, 37, 39–40, 47
Republicans (later Democratic party), 18–19
Revels, Hiram R., 36
Revolutionary War, 8, 10, 11–12, 30, 90
Rhode Island, 6, 25–26, 31
Roosevelt, Franklin D., 91
Roosevelt, Theodore, 76

Sedition Act, 19
Senate, 14, 80–81, 85, 96
Seneca Falls Convention, 58–59
Seventeenth Amendment, 14
Sixteenth Amendment (Anthony Amendment), 67, 69, 76–82
Slavery, 20, 30–32
Smith, Margaret Chase, 85
South Carolina, 6, 11, 12, 24, 30, 31, 34, 37, 39, 52
Stanton, Elizabeth Cady, 58–59, 60, 61, 65
State elections, 14
State suffrage laws, early 1800s, 19–27
Stone, Lucy, 61, 65
Supreme Court decisions, 1, 23, 40, 42, 44–50, 66, 94

Taxes: colonial, 11, 12, 15; early 1800s, 21, 23–26; poll, 42, 45–47
Television, 2
Tennessee, 31, 33, 51, 81–82
Texas, 31, 42, 47, 48, 51
Truth, Sojourner, 61–63
Turnout, voter, 2–3, 97
Twelfth Amendment, 19

Twenty-Fourth Amendment, 47
Twenty-Sixth Amendment, 90, 96

United States v. *Classic*, 48
United States v. *Cruikshank*, 42
Utah, 69

Vermont, 20, 30, 31
Vietnam War, 93
Virginia, 8–9, 10, 25, 31, 47, 52, 90
Voting rights: of blacks, 29–55, 63, 64, 66–67; colonial, 5–15, 18; Constitutional system, 13–15, 18; early 1800s, 18–26; of women, 1–2, 57–87; of young, 89–97
Voting Rights Act (1965), 45, 52, 53, 93
Voting Rights Act (1970), 93–94

Washington (state), 76
Washington, George, 2, 18
Wesberry v. *Sanders*, 1
White League, 38
White primary, 47–49
Williams v. *Mississippi*, 42, 46
Wilson, Woodrow, 76–80
Wisconsin, 36
Women's vote, 1–2, 57–87; and ERA, 83–84; 19th century struggle for, 58–69; 20th century struggle for, 72–82; and women politicians, 84–87
World War I, 78, 80, 91
World War II, 46, 49, 84, 91
Wyoming, 67–69

Youth vote, 89–97